Author's Note:

"Lee Who Stung" is a disguised figure. Some names and details in my reports have been changed. "Your Business" and "None Of" and "Shelly" are not the real names of those persons. Other names and initials may or may not be the actual names of persons involved. These essays are nonfiction for poetic purposes only. They may also be considered fiction, since the past no longer exists. The author sees imaginatively into her life and wishes to respect the privacy of people portrayed who may prefer to remain anonymous.

Acknowledgments

Versions of some of these essays have appeared elsewhere: "A Week in the Life of Alice" and "The Deadline is Now July 21st" in Seattle Review, "The cars She Drives" in The Queen City Review.

Thanks to: Marc Awodey, Ross Conrad, Ruth Eckles, Margaret Jordan, Sally and Bob Eckles, Ana and Thea Price-Eckles, Jonathan Lethem, Rebecca McClanahan, Nora Mitchell, David Shields, the folks from the Bread Loaf Writer's Conference and the Gettysburg Review Writer's Conference, The Vermont Studio Center, Island Arts, and all my students, teachers, and classmates past, present, and future. I thank you all for encouragement and helping kindness.

ISBN 978-0-578-03271-9
Copyright 2009 by Alice Eckles
First edition, first printing

A Phrase Book For Spiritual Emergencies

Essays
by Alice Eckles

The Minimal Press
Burlington, Vermont

ESSAYS

Assessing The Situation
Part One

A Week In The Life Of Alice	11
The Cars She Drives	22
My VNB	31
A Betrayal	41
He Has Her Number Now	45

Gathering Fragments of Desire
Part Two

Piano Lessons	57
O.K. Dudes Fasting	63
Summer	70
Mastery	78
The Race	94

Living With Full Spectrum Communication
Part Three

October, A Short Mystery	104
November	121
Holiday Message	137
Ice Fishing	141
The deadline is Now July 21st	145

Conclusion

Phrases to Use for Spiritual Self-help	160

Part One
Assessing The Situation

A spiritual emergency often goes unnoticed. What could be more normal than constant complaining, or resigned silence about unfulfilled dreams? We are taught that only a few lucky stars will make it big in this world. A spiritual emergency must be recognized as the root cause of failure to accomplish dreams. This book supposes that the spirit is very sensitive to language. The spirit can be drawn out with language so that the emergency can be discerned, and once found the spiritual emergency can be treated with words. This book should not be used as a substitute for professional treatment in an emergency. This book is only an excuse for me to tell you my stories. At the end of this book you will find perhaps some of the more helpful phrases to say or sing to yourself during your own spiritual healing at your discernment of course. The phrase that inspires me to complete this book is: "Help yourself then help someone else." I came upon the phrase while retelling a dream. In the dream it was very windy and I was walking my bike. The wind was so powerful I didn't think it was possible to ride my bike. Then I thought that maybe if I tried I could ride with the wind, so I tried and to my amazement I was riding on air, flying on my bike. Then I came to a little girl who was walking her bike along and I stopped and helped her, making an adjustment on her bike so that she could ride the wind too.

Much of the verbal luring that you can do to get your spirit to come out and be seen is in the form of studying yourself. To describe yourself you have to be observant and interested in yourself. This interest and observation is healing in itself. It feels like a shower of attention. Even if you observed someone else and they didn't know they were being observed, they would benefit. All interest is felt as love. I want to caution you that it is important to be honest in your study. Don't try to simply frame everything as positive. Be frank and let your thoughts flow freely, observing your thoughts as they pass. Try reversing any reoccurring negative thoughts and using the reversal as a mantra. If you often find yourself thinking, "I'm so worried", then try "I don't have a care in the world". The conversations we have with ourselves are important. The words that we say silently, out loud, or sing to ourselves effect us deeply. Language is a mental self-control used for directing and changing behavior. The author is the authority.

What happens in the study of a person is that a path is made, a path that the truth can walk down. The path is not made of truth it is made for truth. Do not worry what the path is made of, make it of everything, use what you have. A sense of humor is important. Only when the self comes walking down the path can you adorn it with encouraging words. My stories are my path. Oddly a mean story if observed from life can draw a person out, like a memory, because we remember the pain.

1

I just wanted to draw a face with good proportion and shading as an example for my elementary art students. I have studied art and created art for years and years, but I never liked working with pastels. They are so dusty and hard to apply exactingly. My collection of pastels offered a limited palette, so I didn't concern myself with realistic flesh tones. My first step is always choosing three tones, a light, a medium, and a dark. I chose tan, yellow and brown. I used tan to fill in the entire face and neck. Brown was my dark tone. I used it to put in the shading indicating the features and shape of the face. With a sort of Naples yellow I put in the highlights.

Turning to my own face in the mirror was the only reasonable way to proceed studying "the face". Not that I was interested in myself, not that I really wanted to capture my likeness.

I didn't care that much what I would look like in the picture. I chose violet and black to get more definition in my eyes, nose, and mouth. I knew it was the wrong thing to do. I knew with my fair skin it would make me look like a zombie, and why should I have to smile to make myself presentable anyway?

How can I begin to describe myself with gentleness, as someone I approve of and love?

A Week in the Life of Alice

First I am not the star and then I throw mud on myself and skulk off to a corner lamenting that I was not the star.

What if I just cut off my head! Wouldn't it be thrilling to live by my heart? Why not just move toward what I want, rewrite my past, like that time I was hiding in the curtains and no one even missed me.

I am tied to my keyboard, because we cannot be trusted to stick together. So, we are strapped to each other in a hope of overcoming a stubborn unwillingness to work together. It has worked with other teams, the monkey and the organ grinder. Out of necessity they learned to cooperate to make music. Out of their being strapped together they found friendship, a livelihood.

I wonder then if I will ever learn to get along with this instrument, or even myself: the reason for this instrument. I never learned to type. A small orange stands on my desk to protect against negativity. If I knew other charms to better my chances I would try them. The sun has not yet come up. My dreams still show the small parts of themselves that stick out from behind my life. Tied to my keyboard, I try to take up my trade again, but mostly I am just drinking tea.

The keyboard is hungry for real collaboration, but I am not very attentive, I could easily just stare and drink tea. I will eat the orange and use its peel to dispel negativity with a spray of citrus scent. Wouldn't we all line up for help if it was a bagful of grapefruits and oranges?

My missing livelihood is taunting and distracting me. There is something natural that is supposed to happen with a writer and a keyboard. The words should naturally flow with beauty, meaning, sound, and imagery. From the spinning of words weaves the clothing of the soul. Without self-adornment, do we exist? The nakedness of my situation, my unclothed soul, my empty beggar's cup, is such a worry that I resent my words and curse them for not being profitable. Here I am with my keyboard. I place the words, but trust cannot easily be regained. The course of nature is to keep its promise. Even a small hope is bound to grow. Things die, without the connection of hope. I sent my wedding ring back five years after the divorce. I sent it back to make room for a new possibility.

I once loved my work. There was reason to believe I was a writer. Then I went on a killing spree. I knew how to do it, how to break bonds and be free, how to clear everything out of my path, how to put a hope to death and move on. I was so adept at moving on that I couldn't keep still, even if I wanted to. I finally settled on a man I had met through the personals ads. I loved him, and did not want to kill the promise. I wanted to renew other promises, like finishing the novel I started a year and a half ago. It is hard to repair a bond that has been broken. I have not touched the novel in 6 months. The disconnection and impending death could not be more obvious. Love is simply an agreement. It can be easy or difficult, but it is just a choice to live in relationship. By strapping this keyboard to my knees I am hoping the choice will be obvious.

I have all the ease of living alone and none of the daily assistance of living with a partner. For a long time I have wanted this solitude, this freedom, but I am not thriving in it. There should be a phrase book for emotional and spiritual emergencies. People, especially teachers like myself, could just speak from the phrase book as needed.

After this time everything had to be cleaned, each night I would tackle a new item in the house. I helped a boy wash a book with a toothbrush, toothpaste and a damp cloth. We had to work quickly and carefully so that the book wouldn't dissolve into pulp. Pulp fiction. I carefully dusted the metal frame of a twin bed kept for guests. Time, whether pure or impure, whether disastrous or productive, brings a web of unclarity and disuse upon the home and its operations. It's as if everything had to be re-found under the sludge of a receded flood. There had been no flood, had there? Could I have been sleeping?

It occurs to me that my house has no foundation, and is merely propped up on cinder blocks. If this fifth great lake should rise and overtake my lawn, my house might just float away. I am used to sleeping with the violence of the winds, and the crashing of the waves. These sounds, that perhaps should be alarming, are my lullaby. Rocked to sleep I could wake up in another place, perhaps not too far away. If the lake took my house for a sail, left me out on newly formed ice, I might leave the house one morning for my usual place of work, never knowing of the change. Maybe in an alignment of small and improbable miracles I wouldn't even notice. My house might be rescued before I returned home, without my knowing, by those ever-ready volunteers on the island I live on. They could have it put back before I got home. "If you get yourself into a bind, call me," the electrician says when I see him at the dump. "If you get yourself into a situation, remember where I live," a neighbor tells me, stopping his car in the road so we can talk. Everyone waves, everyone is friendly. Almost everyone. It's as if everyone is on the team, involved in the secret society of the Volunteer Rescue Squad. They know everything, they know what is at the bottom of the lake, and what is not. They know the exits between exits, the smallest most unknown village.

    A newcomer like myself lives blindly in the unknown, often too embarrassed to ask for help, or too ignorant to know I need it. This is the amusement of the secret society of volunteer rescue people on the island, real islanders, who are not ashamed of their own folly. For example: backing a truck into a tree, sinking a snowmobile by driving fast over the slightly frozen lake. These things are the entertainment of the community. Life can be dull, without the great need of rescue operations.

    Oddly enough, one of the typical Vermont personalities, the kind of Vermonter who is seriously self-sufficient and fiercely independent, is not in stock here on the Champlain Islands. That type of rugged personality formed a hybrid with The Island Personality. The Island Personality is softened by the balmy winds that blow ease into a persons' mind. Island people don't worry so much. We all came here to escape our worries, we all came here to find paradise, often after some trauma, or perhaps just overwork. Sometimes the source of migration goes back many generations. People don't come here so much to escape the city and get back to the land with high ideals like in the rest of Vermont. They come here because they need the therapy of the water to soothe their losses, or simply to fish. They come here to relax, not to return to the land. We have island time, and island bookkeeping, we are a little goofy. Take ice fishing. If there is some ice, someone will try parking a truck on it no matter how early and thin. That's o.k.. That opportunity to put the rescue team to work makes life worth living. We are bonded by our follies. I think in the isolation, after the summer people leave and you realize that you are one of 810 people living on 46 square miles surrounded by water, you lose perspective on issues of personal safety. It is hard to gauge the size of a risk in this half abandoned rural neighborhood. I once called 911 because my carbon dioxide detector didn't seem to be working. Many trucks came speeding, sirens and all, down the potholed little lane where I live. Turned out I needed new batteries. I had never called a neighbor, and certainly not 911, for much bigger emergencies, like when I almost froze to death. Like I say, it is hard to gauge the size of a risk out here, and I am learning that there is something beautiful about that, and about the shared experience we have of that here on the Islands. I really existed after I made that call. Sort of like a numbered joke in prison.

    A phrase fell out of place. "Will you love me?" she asked. She had been here before, not the same place but at a very similar door. He did not know anything about the phrase, he did not know where it came from. What was hiding under it seemed like some sort of code. The code would open the door he very much wanted to open, again. "Yes. I want to make love to you, I want you to make love to me." -pause- "It is hard NOT to love you." That seemed to do the trick, but he didn't know why he had to answer the question. Did she think he didn't love her? Why? Why did she stop and look at him that way?

    No one passes this point without meeting with the question, without answering it. One man lied. He knew what to say and he said it. She heard it and the door opened wide, her heart on view as never before. Some say whatever will open the door. The door is not where it appears to be. One may think they have already been through it, but still the door is there, unopened.

She is wondering how, if his answer had been in written form, it would be punctuated. After he said, "Yes," she took that as one sentence. By the time he got to the rest, "I want to make love to you and you to make love to me," they were already making love, so that part seemed obvious. Then he seemed to add the last, "It's hard not to love you," as an after thought. Was "yes" one sentence? Or was it modified with sexual references? Just a simple yes would have been nice.

She is struggling to understand a new word written on the board. The word, which starts with an "S," changes subtly when a suffix is added. She thinks she understands the word without the suffix but after reading it with the suffix, she gets mixed up. The teacher tries to explain it, going back to the origin of the word, but as she does this, she seems to get lost and unsure of what she knows. Meanwhile the class demands attention. A little girl making a mandala, has covered her circle with the hair that fell off her brush, and now she is on the verge of tears because the teacher took her layers of wet hair, glitter, and little colored balls off the mandala, put them in a shapeless pile on the table - telling her to start over! The teacher is scrambling to avoid the tears that she now sees are near on the girl's face. There is no greater failure for an art teacher than to make a student cry in class.

A lie when it is vivid and alive can make you so aware of the truth that you can no longer tolerate the lie. Betrayal can lure the real gold out of its shell. Once you know your own worth, through betrayal, well, you want to break all connections that are not made with true love. You want to secede from the union and use only real gold and silver for money. If my natural currency is devalued even slightly, it is only a small step to being disposable. Did you ever feel, after having been very close to someone and emerging unharmed, that this person would have tossed your life into the fire if it came to that? How, when I am totally broke, can I begin to change my dealings from false money to exchanges of things with real value?

Yesterday I went to the bank and restructured my debt. I almost forgot the appointment, but remembered it just in time get to there if I left immediately. So I left. The roads were icy and I almost missed the appointment anyway. Afterwards I put together a care package for my daughter who is sick in New Orleans, where she is helping victims of hurricane Katrina. I had put some things from home in a box including: honey, multivitamins, three cans of soup, and some peanut-butter cookies homemade with whole wheat and honey. Then I bought garlic, goldenseal, Echinacea, and acidophilus pills at the Co-op with a gift card my still very new boyfriend gave me for Christmas. I took all this next door to UPS and sent it by two-day mail. I felt that this was not a time to be thrifty even though I was broke. The whole deal came to 80 bucks. I wondered if I was doing the right thing. This is where I go into debt. My parents wouldn't have done such a thing. Not that they didn't care about me, but they weren't unreasonable about it; they had sense enough not to go beyond their means. I always feel when it comes to my children that it doesn't matter what it costs, it only matters that they get everything they need. My extravagant love must go on.

Later at my after school art class we made potato prints and paintings with water-soluble oil pastels. At the end there was still one little girl who had not been picked up. We made a picture on the black board together with colored chalk, taking turns, each adding something new. The picture started out abstract, inside an ornately drawn frame, but eventually it turned into a girl. Her arms were open so wide that they expanded beyond the picture frame, she was smiling but there were also tears coming down. There was a fish in the sky and two butterflies. She had a pet cat nearby. The cat had whiskers on cheeks and eyebrows. The last detail added were two somewhat limp daisies in her hand. Then she left and I carried my box of art stuff to my car and left also. At one point the snow blew across the plains and over the road so thickly that for a few moments the road was not to be seen. The Island is thin and flat, the wind blows where there are no houses or trees, straight over from the West shore to the East shore. Under the bridge chunks of slush gather in a jostling crowd. At home I heat up leftover chicken and potatoes in the toaster oven, I listen to "Switchboard" on the radio, I call T. to see how she's feeling, I take a shower, I read my book, I call S. I finally say what I want to say when it's time to say goodbye. "I love you."

"Thanks," he says. Then a while later, "I love you too."

"Thanks," I say.

My red shoes were somehow still in the grocery store when I left. I didn't buy anything, just looked with admiration and desire at the sweets and the salty sea creatures. I had no money, but I still weighed each temptation carefully. Most important was what I had when I walked into the store, my shoes. Without my shoes, I was nobody, a street urchin. I went running back through the rain for my shoes. My shoes are bright red, made of tough leather stapled to wooden clogs. They are not the kind of shoes you can wear on any job. It is hard to find work that matches your shoes. My friend, M, was in the parking lot unloading her groceries, probably wondering how it could take me so long when I hadn't even bought anything. The important thing was not whether I bought anything but just that I went shopping with my friend, M.. So many things we have to do on our journey, a journey that always seems to have layovers and nights in hotels where you would rather not be and long drives alone that seem senseless; the important thing is that I was with a friend. Some times you can be so lonely and feel grim; meaninglessness can creep up over the cluttered rim, especially when you have to do too many stupid things alone. For this I could start to cry, for this is too much if it happens, the growing darkness, the miles before home, the lack of connection at this time.

It is hard to sit here writing this morning because I went cross-country skiing for the first time yesterday, just by myself. I experimented with falling down a lot, and found that it is very difficult to get back up with skis on. If I had been very careful, I could probably have avoided falling down, but I learn like a child, as if falling down was easy, as if my youthful vitality was made for this abuse, not as if my bone density were declining. I feel now some bruises and sprains, or at least aches and pains. I was glad to be by myself to discover these things; I would not want to be left in the dust. My skiing has a story, sort of, and this is the end of it. I bought these skis, boots, and poles for $100, my mom paid me back and called it a Christmas present. It finally snowed this strangely warm winter, and I skied to the mail boxes at the end on my lane, and thought, "This could be fun." It is an outdoors kind of activity that can be shared, or not. The beginning of my skiing story was a mirage, a hope of love and companionship that sprung up spontaneously like a vision of water in a desert that is not really there.

See my hot air balloon collide with a tall building, the silk flattens as if melting down the side of the building, and our heroine climbs down the fire escape.

I've thought of selling this house. I don't want to, but perhaps it's the only way out of my debt and decline. I bought it as a camp and renovated it to be my year-round home, increasing the value quite a bit. I could pay off my debt and still have some money left to start over. It's just that I'm tired of starting over, and I don't know if I could ever get it this good again, and I need it to be this good. I need to have a place for my children and my parents to visit me. I've been here three years, finally establishing myself somewhere after losing everything in divorce, again. I've been searching for jobs, changing jobs, and trying to find something that really works, constantly for six years. I finally found teaching jobs on the island even though it is not full time, not enough money to live on. I've been living on credit cards. I could sell my house, pay off my debt, and convert my remaining funds into silver and gold, then write my will and check out. I could use my remaining funds to join forces with my still very new boyfriend and make the same mistakes again.

The unbearable truth is that there is no filler, no meaningless, matter-less moment we can have to ourselves that is not chalked up somewhere. It can be hard to breathe when you know this. If it is not I who runs my blood, and breathes my breath, then who? There is someone under the cloth of this reality, it is not only me. Without me, I go on breathing, walking, following my life. There is such a thing as making a choice, but people also pick their scabs not allowing them to heal.

It is not I who catches myself when I fall, but sometimes it is I who throws my self down. I'm trying to catch myself in the act. If I mock anything it is the process of everything. I mock it because I have some kind of issue with it. I feel certain, partly from memory, that everything should happen effortlessly, magically. I especially feel this as an artist. I feel I know, even though everyone says practice makes perfect and I myself have only experienced that there is no free lunch, that things can come fully formed and perfect, that this glorious beauty in all its manifold manifestations is ours to express at anytime. Yet I can't even play the clarinet.

I can listen to the clarinet. I can marvel at the whimsical changes in its voice. I can also watch a moonbeam dance; I see no reason why I cannot actually be that moonbeam, or play the clarinet. If I can actually be a moon beam I do not see why I cannot play basketball in a most compelling way, but only occasionally, if I please. I don't see why one should have to train to be an athlete. I don't see why we have to have such crude processes for painting, writing, weaving, dancing, or surviving. I have this memory of everything happening magically from my brush: whole scenes would appear in one stroke, colors came from plain water. Why now have all the higher automatic processes been taken away from me? I am left with breathing, and the beating of my heart, and a few other automatic responses that come situationally. So I stop mid-blink and try to see just how the automatic, effortless, magical things happen.

I also want to think about it, I want to understand my existence. It just seems like I am here to get imprinted, as if the memories of the world need fresh frontiers like me for storage space. Little bits of consciousness like myself have to break off, get washed, and remake the universe in their own little chip. The process of life is to transfer information into fresh media spaces so that in this redundancy nothing is lost and all is remade. Life is an opportunity to be part of creation by the way that one preserves and arranges impressions. Each person, all life, is the renewal and preservation of creation, making it what it is.

My mission is "to be." This is a service to the godhead and myself. It is strange that we also have to survive and make a living and that we can't just make things happen with a snap of our fingers. That is very strange, but I guess my having been denied access to all that ready-made glory signifies a need to create access, to rebuild piece by piece what was once a flowing whole.

2

In a study of yourself, attention is drawn to what is not right like the hands of an intuitive masseuse. In the next essay, The Cars She Drives, I use a history of all the different cars I've owned to expose my history. Once you have assessed your own progression through life by telling your story by way of anything that has moved along with you in life, you will see what state you are in. This is one of the narrative techniques for dealing with a spiritual crisis. I call it the companion's report.

The Cars She Drives

This covers her life from ages 23 to 41, via all the cars she has ever owned. It starts out in North Bennington, Vermont, during the first Gulf War. Eight cars over 18 years, she has never had the same car for three full years in a row. She is not lucky with cars, but everyone knows that used cars don't last forever. She feels lucky just to get from one used car into the next.

It is after the woman separates from her husband that she inherits the Ford Escort, indirectly. Her sister R. gets the Ford first, after grandmother's memorial service. Apparently it has not been driven for some time because the wheels do not turn when it leaves the driveway, skidding down the steep hill into the village. Sister R. moves in with the young mother and her daughters, so they share the car. Sister R. is from North Carolina, and after a year she decides Vermont is not for her. When R. returns to North Carolina, the car stays behind. Now the young mother drives the Ford Escort all the time, but she is still kind of afraid of driving, especially to strange places, on big highways, or at night. The Ford Escort is not the kind of car that makes you want to drive. It is sluggish and does not like to go up hills. It only has two doors, so she must be careful not to hurt her back as she moves the front seat forward to swing the baby in and out of the car seat several times a day.

    This is the car that makes a driver out of her. Now that she has a car and can drive, her ex-husband asks her to share equally in the transporting of the kids back and forth. She gets used to her route from North Bennington, Vermont, to Keene, New Hampshire, and feels secure as long as it is always the same. In other words, she knows only this road. She doesn't know that all highways are basically the same; she just knows how to get from here to there. A policeman pulls her over as she winds through a valley that is sometimes very foggy; some people refer to this as "going over the mountain." The policeman explains that he pulled her over because she was "weaving," and he is just checking to see if she is o.k.. She assures him that she is o.k..

    Then one day the car really does not want to go up a hill, or even where it is flat. Still she manages to get the car pretty close to home. The Ford Escort dies right in front of Redeemed Repair. She does not know about oil changes yet. She has heard of "tune-ups," but that seems silly and expensive to her. Like car insurance, it can't possibly be a legal requirement! It's a free country, right? They can't make you buy things.

    Her sculpture teacher from England recommends a Buick. "Cheap and good with lots of room to haul whatever you need for sculpture," she said. "My first car was a Buick Skylark, had it for years." So the young mother pays a few hundred dollars for a Buick Skylark at Redeemed Repair. The Skylark has four doors. It has room for hauling kids and sculptures. She drives it to and from Bennington College, parks right next to VAPA, the visual and performing arts building, in an illegal parking place that the

Buick is once forcefully removed from. She parks also in the Bennington Early Childhood Center parking lot, where her girls go to preschool. She has a shameful incident in that parking lot, which she never mentions. Maybe on top of everything the middle aged respectable parents know about her, like that she is too young, too poor, and too divorced to be a good mother, they probably also know that she is the one with a big fat Buick that is always late to pick up her children, and who would try to squeeze herself into the last remaining parking space, hit some other car in the headlight and say nothing since no one sees her do it, then go get her kids and leave before anyone notices. The Buick has no class, and she has no shame.

    She drives impulsively. What she does not know at this time is that her whole life is impulsive. The Buick cuts people off, doesn't know the conventions, goes left on the roundabout. The president of the college actually stops her once as she is going down the wrong side of an island and asks her why she chose to go left, and then goes on to explain that when it comes to driving it is better just to do what people expect, otherwise there could be an accident. "Conventions are useful in driving," she clarifies. Most people think this is just her radical driving style, and most people in this environment tolerate radical styles. Lacking control, she maintains pride in her natural drive, and whatever results.

    One night, she picks up two college age girls hitchhiking, not her age of course, normal college age. She takes them to the next exit where they want to go. It is pouring down rain. After she drops them off the rain pours down even harder, the highway is partially underwater. Her little girls are in the backseat, playing with a tape-recorder. It's a long drive and they like to listen to stories on tape. A., the eldest daughter, says she can't reach a tape that has fallen on the floor. So the young mother takes one hand off the wheel and reaches back while driving to fetch it. At that moment the Buick leans over into the shoulder. Since the shoulder is nothing but water, the car loses contact with the road and begins to spin out of control. "Mom?" four-year-old A. calls out urgently. The young woman is now focused on driving, though the word "driving" doesn't seem to mean anything now. She says firmly, "Everything is going to be all right." They swerve and they slow, then they spin 180 degrees, and land not too roughly with the front passenger side dented from contact with a guardrail. The car has stopped itself, which seems like a blessing. Not knowing what to do next, the woman tries the key. The car turns on and she drives to the next exit. There she finds a service station, and some men who use a coat hanger and rubber bands for a temporary repair till they get home. She drives home in the pouring rain, driving in a new way.

    The Buick was never fashionable, though she thinks it is fine, but now that it has this disfigurement people call it ugly. The woman does not think that looks matter when it comes to cars, but her boyfriend says she should get a quality car, like a Volvo. So she does, and over time comes to realize that he is wrong. The Volvo is a pain in the ass. Always needing expensive and mysterious repairs. Finally so mysterious and expensive that she just gives up on it.

    Nonetheless she takes his advice again and buys a red VW Quantum. Her older sister generously provided funds for this purpose, supporting her decision to go to graduate school. This car teaches her to drive fast. It has turbo, and she has long commutes to graduate school, and to the noncustodial parent's house. While driving her girls to their dad's house she blows a tire going seventy-five miles an hour. She knows how to change a tire, but is shaken and glad when a nice man stops and helps. This is the car that gets her through Antioch New England Graduate School's Accelerated M. Ed. Program, driving from Montpelier, Vermont to Keene, New Hampshire once a week. With this car she leaves the boyfriend who watches her kids while she spends two days a week at Antioch. She goes to live with someone else, whom she later marries. Her new husband, like her last husband, drives a stick shift, and his car is converted to run on vegetable oil. He is the father of two little girls, who are friends of her two little girls.

The VW Quantum has a window that will not go up and down, it is propped up inside the door with a two by four. Water leaks into the car from some mysterious hard to find place under the dash, which makes the car smelly, damp, and unpleasant. The electrical gizmos never work but are expensive to repair, and easier to do without. As if by providence, the VW Quantum is totaled at Greensboro Garage in Hardwick, where her car is waiting to be repaired. An elderly couple slides off the icy black tar of Route 14 and right into her red VW Quantum in the lot. The old couple takes full responsibility, and their insurance pays for her next car, a grey Subaru.

The grey Subaru takes her growing children to The Green Mountain Waldorf School in Wolcott from East Calais. The woman's children have grandparents on their father's side who also live in Vermont on Putney Mountain, and they've always had Subarus. She reasoned that Subarus with four-wheel drive must be good Vermont out-in-the-booneys type cars. The woman now lives in a log cabin in the woods with her new husband. She does not like getting stuck out there in the wilderness alone, so she wants four-wheel drive. The father of her children moves to Northampton Massachusetts, so there is a monthly trip to Northampton. He has them every other weekend, and they take turns with the driving.

This is the car that she learns to trust her judgment in, the car that no one can make her drive if she feels the roads are unsafe. The car of measured risks. She often feels pressure from her ex to drive the kids in scary snowstorms, and freezing rain. She develops her own method of deciding if the roads are safe. She calls ICY-ROADS, she looks at the forecast, she inspects the car, and calculates the hours of daylight.

One day impatience, impulsivity, and anger overcome her. There is some kind of bad mood in the house, maybe cabin fever, but she just wants to get away from her husband. One of his daughters starts throwing a fit. The woman feels it all has to do with some sort of unpleasantness coming from her husband. She wants to get the kids in the car and go - do something fun like ice skating - quick. The girls are in a bad mood, which makes the woman want to press on the gas. The roads are very icy, but she hasn't checked the roads, or the weather. The woman and the four girls just pile into the car and drive off as if it were a normal day, backing out of the driveway and going down the hill in a carefree way. Soon it becomes clear that this is not a normal day but a winter weather advisory day. "Shit" she says, as the steering fails to work on the ice, as if she already sees in her mind's eye exactly what is going to happen. She presses the brakes, avoiding one thing to hit another. Better a slow hit from behind than a fast hard blow up front, she reasons, knowing that when you use the brakes on ice steering is nonexistent.

    The back end of the grey Subaru crashes into the trunk of a big tree. She gets out, shovels the snow from under the tires, throws down some ashes she keeps for this purpose and with a little rocking back and forth, the car is free. They continue into town and go skating. After that, the Subaru doesn't pass inspection anymore, and she found that replacing a back door was almost undoable. So that was the end of that car.

    A white Subaru replaces the grey Subaru. This is the car for the smoldering complexity of passion, anger and destruction. This woman is driven, but the events of her life swallow every car like a beast, ripping their identities off the pages of history. This car is a chariot of fire, and all that that implies. The woman and her new husband finish building an addition to his workshop by the road. Now each child has her own room, and the woman has her own art studio. She has a mysterious bad feeling in her gut. This she cures by walking and writing everyday. The children are happy. The woman keeps a garden that no one goes to because it's far away. She plants hazelnut trees that actually produce nuts. The woman begins to have art shows, she starts a fortune cookie business, she starts an email correspondence writing long notes to an art critic every day. She forms this email correspondence into a book titled <u>My Life As A Flower</u>. She publishes it as a hand bound edition of fifty books. She begins NOT to admire her husband who she admired so much in the beginning for his self-sufficiency in the Vermont landscape. Not as self sufficient as he seemed, she thinks. Neglectful, she thinks. She does not want to take care of him, and she does not want him to take care of her, not in the ways that they have been. At first he wants a divorce, then he wants her to stay and be his wife. She is either earning her keep, or undeserving of it. At first she does not want a divorce, but then she refuses to stay after he has toyed with her options.

    They can't stand each other's presence anymore, it all happens very quickly, all in the month of August. She and her children pack up in a week. The 15th of August passes. Their 5th anniversary, if they had celebrated it, passes without mention.

    The white Subaru is filled with her stuff. She alone moves to Burlington. Her first ex, her children's father, picks up the girls in a big white van that they fill with their belongings. She decides that she will not go on welfare to support her daughters, that she couldn't bear it again, so she sends them to live with their dad, who is not the one she is divorcing this time. That's how they move to Northampton Mass. The younger daughter at fourteen will not pack up any of her things in protest of the move. "I am happy here," she says.

    The white Subaru filled with the woman's last load of belongings mysteriously catches fire at night while parked in the driveway at a friend's house in Burlington. The fire truck comes and waters down the ashes. Burnt letters lie wet and plastered to the drive. She has to pick through this and decide what to keep, what to toss. Some very fragile Christmas tree ornaments survive the car fire, the Santa has soot on his face now, everything else is lost.

A Suzuki ushers her into a new life as a certified and practicing art teacher. She is looking for an automatic, four wheel drive, hatchback, with a roof rack, 4,000 dollars or less, preferably White, under 100,000 miles, and not older 10 years. She loves the Suzuki; it is her most favorite car ever. The Suzuki does not come to a violent end like most of her cars, the Suzuki simply rusts out.

For the next car, a Kia Sportage, she goes to the same dealership, The Imported Car Center. She wants to get a car just like the Suzuki since she had been so happy with it. The Kia has fewer miles on it than any car she has ever owned in the past. She hopes it will last a lot longer. Icy Roads are less of a worry now because of global warming.

However she discovers after only a year and a half of owning the Kia that she really can't afford to own a car, not the Kia with its high maintenance costs, not with gas at $3.69. She discovers the reason her personal economy isn't working. It's because of her car. She points the finger at this thing in her life. The car is the hole in her pocket that she needs to mend. It's not easy selling the car that summer as everyone else is discovering the same thing in their lives. Finally in August she sells the Kia for thousands of dollars below book value to a dealer. For transportation she shares her boyfriend's car and his truck, he has converted both to run on used vegetable oil. She does not live with her boyfriend they are many miles apart. This is not exactly a solution but it does mitigate the problem since it costs less to borrow a car than to own one and used vegetable oil is currently cheaper than gas.

Maybe I should embrace my racing heart of horror. This story, as I read it in the Queen City Review is percussive, like a mad mother forever chopping vegetables, there is no violin's voice, there is no singing, maybe one wail escapes the pressure cooker just before the last crammed in installment. It moves fast, life as a silver bullet. Cars are not like dogs, they do not comfort, and they do not bring their story into yours as a bond before dying. Cars are machines that take you through life, and it is unfortunate to be taken through life by a machine. The cars seem to highlight her difficulties, only briefly one car seems to represent a small amount of very prized success. In the afterward we learn that she is no longer a car owner and this gives me hope of perhaps a slower, easier, more controlled life: a less risky life on foot. It also speaks of power, and sharing power. It's a mean story. It's not a story filled with gratitude. The only scrap of gratitude is being glad I lived. I don't know why I had to tell such a mean story, I should be tired of telling about my hard life by now. I think it is because I used my cars to move the story. Cars move fast and gratitude moves slowly, like love. Not that love itself is slower than a car, but it can take a while to get to me sometimes. Like gratitude, all along I have much to be thankful for, but the actual thanking is sometimes overlooked.

3

"You always have what I need"

Much of my writing is about my difficulty in identifying friends and community. What makes someone a friend? How is friendship defined? Family members are more defined, than friends but even that can be complicated by divorce. I resort to scavenging the wisdom of others. I listen for what I say that gets repeated, that's how I find my own wisdom. Other people lift out therapeutic suggestions, like needles in the haystack of my verbal dump. Listening for the whisper of flattery they find proverbs. Other people everywhere are speaking from the <u>Phrase Book of Spiritual Emergencies</u> right now. The medicine for optimal performance is being uttered as you pass if you learn to hear it, through the thunder of ... perhaps paranoia? The phrase, "You always have what I need.", came to me like this: I was at a dinner party my grandmother was hosting, and I needed a spoon so I went to the kitchen to get one, on the way there I crossed paths with my sister and she had a spoon which I took saying, "You always have what I need" A phrase I never would have noticed if someone hadn't responded, "What a beautiful way to feel about someone"

Another special phrase came into my life recently:

"All I ask of you is for you to forever remember me as loving you"

I was participating in a Kirtan, an ancient Vedic chanting ritual. At Metta Earth, a center for contemplative ecology, they do their Kirtans a little differently. Instead of chanting traditional foreign phrases after a leader they treat it more like a singing jam session with a few instruments passed around the circle. It's a silly symphonic conversation. It's not always silly of course, but the fact that sometimes it is makes it heart freeing. I didn't think I would like Kirtans and avoided them at first even *though I'm quite involved with the Metta Earth community and they host a Kirtan the second Saturday of every month. I have found the Kirtans to be a fun. A woman sitting to my left suggested with a certain melody that we look across the room and sing to someone in particular "All I ask of you is for you to forever remember me as loving you". I looked across the room to my sweetheart and he was looking at me and we sang it to each other except that I couldn't sing it without tears, and practically losing my voice. The song was easy enough to sing staring at a candle in the center of the room. Why did it make me cry to sing it while looking into my loved one's eyes? It is true that love is the most important thing to be remembered for, and yet consistently I forget, and feel resentful that I am not famous. It seems I ask for much more than to be remembered for loving anyone. I ask instead to be remembered for my contribution to literature, which sounds so small and selfish and so much less of an honor, so much less of a reality than my being forever remembered for loving my friends and family. Maybe the tears came because my resentment against the fame-withholding world blinds me. Through the hurt it is hard to recognize my loved ones at all, much less to remember that love is the only thing I need to be remembered for. Perhaps my art in whatever form it takes is my love and part of the memory forever kept by my loved ones. The woman who offered this song at the Kirtan, is someone I am beginning to especially like. She appreciates me for my "…whimsical deep running thinking." Her appreciation means a lot to me. Her words of appreciation for me are the ones I search so hungrily for, forgetting that I know right where they are. They are inside a card she sent that is magnetically posted to the file cabinet by my desk.*

My VNB

When I tell myself stories about my current life, I refer to him as my VNB. This is an acronym for my Very New Boyfriend. I woke up this morning while he slept soundly next to me, worrying about what I would call him when he was no longer new, like if it became long term, after I had known him for a while and he had known me. Years later, what would I call him? I heard him making sleeping sounds. Suddenly I was at ease again, he would just be my Very Nice Boyfriend, and therefore still my VNB. Even the loss of a silly name is too much. It certainly seems like too much to hope for permanence in a relationship. I am twice divorced. I call him my VNB to keep perspective. I can call him my boyfriend, but I have to realize that he is still very new.

Some of the things I like about my VNB are kind of odd. They are not the kind of things you are supposed to like. I like that he is short; he is just my size, and I am five foot two and only 98 pounds. I'm sure he must have a little more bulk, and he says he is five four, but it seems to me that we are head to head. I usually wear two-inch heels, so maybe he is telling the truth. I would hate to think he is lying about his height, but it wouldn't matter to me if he were only five two. Like me he is well proportioned for a short person, not too stout or too scrawny. I also like the hair on his back. It is long, and very soft and gently curving. I like it when some of it stays in my bed reminding me that he has been there. I like that he was there when I needed him, like when we first met. I had a second date booked with a new person from the Seven Days Personals, but then the guy cancelled our date, and I was not happy about the new empty space on Sunday morning. That is how I met my VNB. He was the replacement, and he made everything work out just right. So now I love him.

My VNB is a beekeeper. I absolutely love honey and have always wanted a direct connection to the source. The first time he came to my house, he was looking around at my things, but I put my hands on him and I pulled him to the couch. Before I saw him again I bought a five-pound jar of honey from a competing apiary. I decided afterwards that this was a challenge. If he were still my VNB after I had eaten all that honey, then he could give me some of his own honey. Then it would be real honey to me.

Today my VNB gave me honey. He gave me a one pound jar of honey and told me he would keep me supplied, that I should save the jars through the winter and come August he would fill them all back up. I said that was definitely the program for me.

My VNB seems very generous, especially if I am in need of any kind. This made me have a revelation: People take care of each other so that they can be together. This seems extremely nice to me. Am I going to have a place that I belong? When you belong really physically with another person, that's the best kind of belonging there is. It's very warm. We only see each other about once a week. I go there Mondays after work and we go out to dinner and then to swing dance classes we are taking together. Not until after that do we get very close and take each other's clothes off. If we get dressed again afterwards, he wears the bottoms and I wear the tops. I love my jellyroll, deep down in my soul. The dance class makes me think about roles, how the dance requires the woman or follower to really stick to that role. I was thinking its like separating your right and left brain and letting one side become dominant so that the two sides can work together, it's like that basic need to chose one hand over the other, rather than being ambidextrous. It's an organizational thing that facilitates connectivity; all these ideas seem at the root of some of my long-standing problems.

My VNB is from Manhattan and maybe that explains why he eats so fast. It may also explain why he is not so easily offended. I apologized for saying that I wasn't sure if his honey tasted better or if it was just because I liked him that I thought it tasted better. He said he is not so sensitive, because he's from NYC. He explains that he meant it as a joke, when he replied that, "No, it's not because you like me, my honey really does taste better." The truth is I am very sensitive and any reply that starts with "No" after I had just said I liked him seemed like, hey-wait-a-minute to me. The truth is he jokes a lot, but I see it as a gentle sparring.

A constant mock fight, a teasing, that helps us get to know each other. So I am bouncing back from his playful jabs but then I am not from NY and I say hey-wait-a-minute, who you call'in lazy? Who you call'in easy? Just joking he says.

On Valentine's Day winter's first huge snowstorm came and stalled all traffic between long distance lovers, me in North Hero, and him in Middlebury. It was as if all that separated us were these chunks of snow, like white frozen cake endlessly between us, more than we could eat, spanning twenty-five villages and two counties. We were probably both shoveling our driveways, as if at opposite ends of a shoveled path. The snow was beautiful while making it difficult to see each other; it was romantic making us think of each other in its beauty. However, a day or two before when I saw him last, he took me shopping for a present of clothes. Shopping for clothes is a very serious and private matter and I have not approved of the more recent development I have noticed of men going shopping with women and standing near the curtain, or flipping through the racks of what might be covering their women shortly. Also I avoid gifts. Unless I am really in love, it is sort of a test. A test that seems more of a true indicator than other things, like sex, or saying I love you. Something in me will not accept a gift, especially a personal and expensive gift, like this soft loosely knit slightly pink angora sweater with rhinestone buttons. I did let him take me shopping and stand by the curtain, smiling when I tried on a little black sweater wrap that I was busting out of, that was fun.

I have his name written on my calendar on November 22nd, but that is a Wednesday, so I know that is not the first time I saw him. The first day I saw him was a Sunday, the 12th I believe. So it has been 14 weeks since I met him, 4 months. I was going to say he is now my Very Nice Boyfriend, but it has only been 4 months. Since then there has been Christmas, New Years, and Valentine's Day. We have celebrated them all together. Our birthdays are in the summer, for which I am grateful. It is not good to have a birthday too soon in a relationship. We don't have an anniversary of any sort. On New Years we went to the place where we first met. Can just saying hello be something to recapitulate? By date three I told him I had eliminated other suitors. Not too long after that I told him, it will only take me a month to decide about you.

"A month from now or from when we met?"

"From when we met."

It's been 4 months and I'm still with him. What I don't know is when his middle name changes from New to Nice. New or Nice, middle names are often not even used. Mine was only used when I was a child, like a tail that followed my name. Perhaps middle names are a sign of immaturity. They fall off like baby fluff when you grow up. Maybe the relationship is growing up, and that middle point is silent, not speaking of change.

I didn't tell you about the colors I saw under my eyelids as I drifted off to sleep in your arms: First came blue puddles of neon water sleeping in the dark. Then something completely different, folds of cream and tan filling my eyes. A tree flower, the kind with a furry shell that falls away, as flowers bloom to the edges, obscuring whatever kind of tree it is. The cream and tan surprised me because I've never had a profound feeling about these colors; they have never come to me in a vision, this soft mixture of whites and browns.

Sometimes I fall into a staring contest. My mind and the world - we cannot let go, nothing happens, time passes, we refuse to move on, it is a seductive nothingness, I am very still.

Colors come like friends to me. They come from my heart, they come to my heart, and they bridge whatever is parted.

I push the hours across in wheelbarrows and go to bed hungry. It seems there is a reason for doing this, but I don't know what it is. Should I prepare for the night with hunger? Should I dispose of night, as if time would not move without being carted away like leaves in fall?

The mulch of one day feeds the next. My hunger awaits the food of dreams. Pushing these last hours over is like putting food by that comes all a sudden at summer's end. As this day moves past its prime my anxieties lose relevance. Nothing more can be expected from this day.

Out of all the uncertainty in this world, it seems like a miracle that I can go to sleep and expect to wake up the next day. I suppose death comes unexpectedly. If I can feel something on the other side of today, if I can feel my life continuing on the other side, then perhaps, too, I could feel death if it were close by. Perhaps in proximity there is certainty.

I love the complete involuntariness of waking up in the morning, I look forward to it, I am grateful for the automatic becoming that enfolds me. I do not want to look beyond this one gift.

"If I have to make a cake," my mother told me holding up a beautiful slice, "this," she said giving me a taste, "is the kind I will make." It was angel food with sliced almonds on top.

Why would my mother "have to" make a cake? I know why, but I am afraid to say.

She didn't ask me what my plans were, it was more like she was warning me of an event that may be approaching. The almonds were very pretty all laid out in rows, like flat cream colored petals outlined in brown, so quiet, holding a symphony on its nutty mantle, a sort of chewy, crunchy candy, complementing the cloud of cake underneath.

She only asked me to taste the cake. I told her it was good. If I don't get married, it will not be for lack of a cake.

Nonetheless, even though she didn't ask me about my plans, her prepared response to a possible situation points to this question.

I plan to help my boyfriend to build a house that I might share. I might not be sure that I want to marry him, and he hasn't asked me. Maybe I do, and maybe he will. In any case he plans to build the house this summer. I get a good feeling when I think about joining him, and he did invite me, so I figured I'd take the chance. If it doesn't work out I still have my own house. If it does work out, there could be a call for cake.

Sometimes, in a moment, everything you need is there and you know what to do with it. We went to a conference. There was a cake celebrating 25 years of the Northeast Organic Farmers Association staring us in the face, several huge one-layer cakes in a few different flavors. I remember pointing out the hazelnut cream cake with special interest rather than the chocolate. I remember how he brought it to my mouth. It felt very ceremonial. And it tasted good.

Someone asked me if I was single recently and I said, "Not anymore." It felt strange.

When sleeping beauty woke up it was very hard for her to get out of the castle because the vines had overtaken the back door. She pushed it open just a crack, and saw the arms of an octopus tree crisscrossing the opening. From the outside probably you could not see the castle at all. The woody arms and creeping tendrils held the door tight to the stone wall, but she pushed herself through what little space she could make. Then she went for a drive in her black car. I don't know where she was going; maybe that's why she pulled over when she saw a wide shoulder where other cars had stopped. She pulled over but the ground was very soft there, it undulated like a carpet being shaken out, causing another car to roll onto hers. Her car was badly damaged. She counted six broken windows and two doors had holes in them. "Clearly this was not my fault" she thought, "I'm sure the other driver will pay for the damage." But the other driver drove off. The keeper of the shoulder was no help either, he said, "No, nothing can be done. You have to take care of it yourself."

In the bed, her boyfriend was away, and an old boyfriend was there. Oops, she must have had an affair.

She was confused at first about whether to be loyal to the old boyfriend since they had been together before, or to her current boyfriend who was away. Then she felt very clear, in a horrible way, that she should be loyal to her current boyfriend, because it was his bed, and his house! How could she have done such a thing! Now she was wondering if she should tell her boyfriend about this when he comes back. If she tells him he may desert her, and who would blame him? If she doesn't tell him that doesn't change what happened, it would just mean hiding something from him.

She woke up; the affair was only a dream, not a very pleasant one. She remembers one particular instant, yesterday, when a man pulled her close, they were dancing. Her boyfriend was dancing with someone else. There was no space between her breast and the stranger's ribs, his hand pressed just below her shoulder blades drawing her into his frame.

I have been thinking about the word "inconclusive." I have found love but it is "inconclusive." Inconclusive? Who decides? Him or me? It seems wise not to jump to conclusions, but I am a jumper, and that is my wisdom. I have jumped into us, and he is uncertain. Sometimes I am wrong, sometimes there is a contrast between what I believe and reality. That contrast can be dangerous.

I have decided not to say I love you during sex anymore. I don't want to start an argument about what love is, or if we are in it, that's the last thing I want to do. I've decided that if I have the urge to say I love you in such a moment, I will just say something like oh-baby-you're-so-hot instead. That certainly would not start an argument. I never say things like that. I only smile. That's how I quell the urge to say I love you. It's like singing "B-I-N-G-O", or "My Hat it has Three Corners", and replacing each word in turn with a clap, until the whole song is only clapped.

There are two stages of conclusiveness. There is a kind of sense-making that happens immediately and automatically when and where a person needs sense, that's my first conclusion. Then there is the time test, a utilization of the sense made, that's the second stage of concluding. One tries to use what one has found and if it works then one can say one has discovered a reality.

I'm feeling the edges of what this is that my heart described in northern lights. I know how it is not to have words for your opinions; it is like having only a spoon to eat with. It is like not having a knife.

I can come to a conclusion. I have given up looking for an echo to confirm my position. I hesitate to state the reasons for my faith. I have given up hearing you echo it; I still believe it is there.

A warm spring day, our first this year, the bees are gathering pollen. I see it on their knees. We are working in the bee yard all day. The warm sun, the buzzing bees, the hours of reversing hives, inspecting and cleaning them, scraping away bees wax, the smell of the bees wax, the taste of the bee's bread, fermented pollen, it makes me drowsy, the sun, the humming. I love working with you. What makes it pleasant is not anything but the way the work flows, the way it is supported between us. It is mesmerizing like the hum of the bees all around me.

It may seem that I picked the wrong stories to illustrate the phraseology native to the self healing mind, but the fact is all my stories address all the topic areas. A native speaker of the inner world does not isolate topics to illustrate how to talk about one specific topic. Yet it is useful to learn a native speaker's poem, exactly because it is not a lesson, only a cultural example. I chose Betrayal to represent "talking about the past" because of the feeling of regret that highlights the very idea of "the past". Until I wrote this story I thought I was so smart when I was an adolescent to exclude myself from the culture of adolescence. After losing my friend, I'll call her Shelly, I decided social life was too difficult. Now I realize that I missed many learning opportunities, stubbornly and unduly, I retarded myself.

Anyhow, you have to establish a rapport with yourself, your high self, your low self, and your intermediary self; that's the foundation for healing communication. Put all your emergencies aside and get calm, put yourself in neutral. Establish authority by writing the whole thing down, and claiming to be on your side, that's your prerogative as the author. Don't lie. Find comfort and entertainment for yourself till you get over it, or help arrives. Avoid going into debt to pay off bad karma. I mean don't make things worse by being hard on yourself.

Betrayal

A betrayal does not have to be big to be effective. One can step to the other side rather quietly, barely moving, shifting just a little; the gesture is the same no matter how small. Alice was about fourteen. Let's back up a year or two. It had taken her a long time to make friends after moving to Fort Scott, Kansas, in the fifth grade. At first she did not even like her friends, they were just the people who grabbed her when she first arrived, and she found it hard to get away from them. Before betraying the true friend she finally found, she betrayed these cling ons, in fifth grade. This, Alice does not regret. It seemed like the only way, although it was shameful, and she is ashamed of it. It was the only way she knew, having seen other girls do it. She put a "kick me" sign on one of the girls in her cluster. It was so effective. These were not friends she had chosen, but were like hitchhikers, stickers that cling to you when you wander across a field. The worst part is, and she did this non-maliciously, she used Elmer's glue to put the sign on the girl's coat while it was hanging with the rest in a row of hooks. She really didn't think of how difficult it would be to get that off, till she saw the white paper in stripes on the corduroy coat the next day. She never took credit for the deed.

Over the summer, having spent sixth grade utterly alone, she luckily made a very important new friend, Shelly. Shelly became her best friend. She lived just down the street from Alice. They spent time at each other's houses every day. Shelly was Catholic and had eleven brothers and sisters. Shelly's big sister gave the two friends a ride to school. Shelly and Alice were such good friends that they knew what the other was just about to say, and would fall into a fit of laughter when they said it at the same time: jinx. Often this happened while eating a snack and milk would laugh right out of Shelly's nose in a spurt, and that made them laugh all the more.

Shelly and Alice had a project, they were designing a house that would be fun to live in. A fun house, with slides instead of stairs. It was an "A" frame. Life was infinitely better for Alice now that she had Shelly as a friend. Shelly had smooth waves of blond hair, and a beautiful smile. She was the youngest in her large family and somehow that gave her a surefooted feeling, she had much support and guidance from her brothers and sisters, perhaps even her priest.

Alice was a little different, and more without support and guidance. She did not really even believe that her mother was the same mother she had when she was younger. Shelly did not believe that Alice was born in New Orleans, because no one in Fort Scott, Kansas, came from a far away unknown exotic place like that. If she had said she was from Hutchinson, Kansas, that would have been believable. Alice always told the truth, sometimes just not enough of it.

After the summer, junior high school started, and Alice noticed the girls at school were different. There were new opportunities for friendship. There was a competitive jostling. It seemed like it had been secretly decided by the other girls, if temporarily, that Alice was cooler than Shelly. Alice did not have any zits, whereas Shelly had a few rather large ones, and was prone to greasy skin.

In the hall a new friend grabbed Alice saying: "We don't want to go to the movies with Shelly anymore because she has zits. It is better to have friends like Susie who will attract cute boys, don't you think? I want to go to the movies with you and Susie but not Shelly. Do you have to invite Shelly? Just this once could you not call her?"

"I guess"

"Don't you think her zits are disgusting, so big and white"?

"Well, I guess"

Shelly heard about all this, and after a few times of not being invited to the movies with the rest of the gang, she perceived that Alice had joined them against her.

On the advice of her older sister Shelly recognized that anyone who would do such a thing was not a true friend. So Alice lost Shelly. After that Alice decided to be a hermit.

She would no longer go to the movies with anyone. She would not even talk in school. So long as she was in this town she preferred no social life at all. She went for long walks alone at night. Shelly's mother said she was a streetwalker.

    Friendships with girls and women always seemed to end badly for Alice. She began to see herself as fickle, lacking loyalty, unable to see social situations clearly. "Women are not as nice," she explained to herself, but then she didn't like men much either. Even though they might be nice, they seemed not as smart. Finally she thought, I am a confused ambidextrous person; never having chosen which hand will lead me, which hand to open doors with, every social move is a bumbling choice or refusal to choose. Why should I choose? Why can't we all go to the movies together? Why can't we all be friends?

Some wise person said, you can understand other people in solitude, but you can only know yourself by interacting with others.

Describing interpersonal relationships is like making your own movie. You have to make your own because the existing culture you find yourself immersed in may not reflect your reality, especially in the romance department. Falling in love is a made up idea, like sending Christmas cards, we don't have to do it to ratify the season. Falling in love is a myth I don't want to buy into. My ideas about love are based on my experiences as I move toward what I want. I want to learn and grow, and yet I find that I can barely tolerate a person who helps me to learn and grow. Learning and growing is not easy, there are growing pains. My partner is like a coach who pushes me, encourages me, and witnesses my successes and failures. On the one hand I'm glad he's there, on the other I can barely stand him. When I throw myself down and cry in frustration, I can barely stand him looking over me, even the thought that he might say something encouraging, yet I'm glad he is there, he makes me feel safe. When I am trying to concentrate he is yelling out helpful hints. I can hardly stand it, but I do because I know he'll understand if I ignore him. Some of the hints if I can bear to hear them might even be helpful.

Personality is not the reservoir of universal love or universal anything. It's the part of you that is very resourceful when it comes to fear. It's the part of you that sins and the part of you that dies and doesn't go to heaven or anyplace else. So I say treasure it, you only live once. Your personality only lives once, your soul is bigger and probably immortal that's something to treasure too.

Describing interpersonal relationships is really quite advanced for Part One of any book. I just felt I had to jump into it, just an instinctive jump.

He Has Her Number Now

Optimism and love, the kind of drink that mothers toss back in anger and sadness with the news of war. I learned to love as a mother, not as a girlfriend, and my allegiance will always be with the younger generation.

"Hi, this is Chris calling"
"Excuse me this is who?"
"Chris ***-****"
"No, ***-6***"
"Oh, sorry."
"O.K., bye."

So he has her number now, if he likes the sound of her voice he can call again. Isn't this like most meetings anyway, where you have so little to go on? It did seem like they wanted to talk to each other though. The phone book for the village is thin; She looks through the numbers till she sees the one he intended to call. Oh, the Ocellos, they have a blue mailbox. She does not know more, she is new to the island.

She lives alone, checks out videos from the library, watches them at night. The movie had just ended and she was singing along with the exit music, "I am calling you" The words stretch out a long time floating in the air. When the phone rang she had just finished singing the phrase.

Relationships are exciting, whether making friends, or perhaps more than friends. Something like that could still happen even without there being any reason for it. She might take a young lover. The problem with being forty is you forget how old you are; you don't realize that a guy you could be attracted to could be your daughter's age. She thinks, I better set an age limit right now. How young is too young? Twenty, she answers, and feels terrible for not saying thirty. Terrible. Lately she notices how older women look great and older men look terrible. It's not just looks; it's the attitude in the looks. Maybe it is a particular male face that comes to mind when she thinks, young lover. Oh, probably. She met a young guitar playing poet, his bohemian teacher brought him to her on a "poetry field trip". He had thick eyebrows, he already admired her, from afar he had heard her. A silly boy, they all are. She is tired of old men. They get old so fast, oh the doddering. A boy, a boy would be nice. Maybe it is one particular boy, is he more than twenty? She is not sure which is worse, the particular or the generality.

*

The professor's annual backyard reading was a summer tradition she had learned about from a friend. She decided to consider herself invited by association and went, with a story about apple picking to read. The professor in his back yard, wearing shorts was remarkably small and childlike. She has a secret concerning this man. For a brief moment she considered being a literary critic, and used his book as a guinea pig. If anyone tried to buy his book on Amazon they would see her review of it. The review was not completely positive; perhaps pooh poohing the whole male experience but it was also a very positive review, if that is possible. So there, he doesn't know this as they stand and look into each other's eyes. They have to be sure what they are seeing, so they look.

She touched his arm to get his attention because she didn't know his name, or felt unsure of it.

"Thanks for inviting me, I think I'm going to go now"

"Thanks for coming, I'll have to invite you again next year. Do you do other readings, like at the Firehouse?"

"Well, I live in North Hero, so no. Thanks, bye"

She noticed his teeth as they talked. They were small and sharp. The moment seemed more intimate than she intended, he seemed younger, his eyes more clear than she expected from a middle aged bald man. How will he invite her to the next reading, he has no contact information? If he did read her review would he be angry? Flattered? Would he think she had a lot of nerve? Sneaking around like that. His eyes had blond lashes.

*

Blond, heavy set, strong, vegetarian, a college boy, came with them to Senegal, Africa, sort of as an apprentice to the engineer, the one she was marrying within days. She and the boy spent a lot of time together because the engineer had work and the apprentice was not always needed.

"Don't you want to come out into the waves? You would love it."
" I'm not a good swimmer, it's too rough for me."
" Come, I'm a trained life guard, if you start to drown, I'll save your life, it's what I'm trained to do."

She didn't feel like starting to drown, but she did feel like humoring him. She thought he could save her life, given the opportunity. She thought it was funny, the offer, and that he seemed to think she should expand beyond her fears. Most Senegalese do not swim. They respect the mighty sea, and go out there only on business, for life sustaining fish.

"O.K. then watch me because I may need to be saved"

She went out into the waves. The boy and the elder engineer loved the waves, spending hours there; The elder engineer, her fiancé, would fall asleep on a boogie board in the ocean. The woman, not going out beyond a certain point saw herself as wiser, like the Africans. She humored the boy and went out beyond where she herself knew she had control. Let the American boy save me, she thought, he can, he's been trained to do it. For two or three waves it was o.k. , but then she was submerged, like a small silk clothe obeying the wind, under and over she went violently toward the shore, rejected by the heavy seas, her swim suit powerfully torn off, filled with sand, bam, on the shore she quickly pulled it back up, crawled to her towel.

"Was it fun?" he asked.
"Yes, pretty fun for a while, but I don't think I will do it again."
He went back out into the waves; she combed the beach for pretty shells.

"You're unconventional." He said.
"How do you know?" she said.
"You don't shave your legs."

There was a good Italian pizza place, Giovanni's, really Italian, it was good. They would go there together sometimes. "There is a girl" he said, "who writes me very long letters, why? See her picture. What does it mean, what does she want me to do?" She shrugged her answer. An angry man, cursing about politics - "You are lucky to be Americans" he tells them. "We have the same corrupt president for thirteen years"

"Come, let's cut my hair. In your room, you have a mirror" he said

His hair was long, thick, sticking out in strands brown and blond twisted together. He shaved too. Got himself a whole new look. She had too, a new look, because some women on the island they went to, the one where the slaves stayed before being shipped off, now a tourist spot, that seems to hold no grudge, they corn rowed her long hair. It was so much more convenient for extended drives in human packed taxis with all the windows open and the wind, the dry wind blowing, the scattered baobab trees like giant jade plants, enchanted figures out there.

    Visiting a village:
    "Do you eat fish?" our host asked
    "Last time I checked fish was an animal," he says

    He is strict, has chosen himself to make the sacrifice of not eating meat. Not everyone has to do this to make the world a better place, but he can so, he will. He does not appear to be too thin, he does not need meat. He has meat on his bones.

    They sit next to each other in the car, bouncing along the road, thighs touching. He is a bicycle guy; improving bicycles will change the world. She enjoys his companionship; she is amused that he thinks he knows what is best for her. He loves his mother, she knows this, and senses the echo. She loves her children; it is the only true love. He is young enough almost to be her son.

    The generation that I love is going to war.

Part Two:
Gathering The Fragments Of Desire

On the way to a place of healing, the king comes to meet me warning small creatures of his approach with a bell on top of his scepter. In his wisdom and fatherly devotion he leads me to the door of a man I was once involved with. "Perhaps you will at least remember what happened if you meet him." The king said knocking on Ian's door. At once I became hopeful and afraid: The mystery of my fate was about to be revealed. Either I was loved, or worthless. Just as the door was about to open I ran away.

I felt ruined, like I had done something terribly wrong. I was in disarray, my blond hair was messed up and I could hardly see because I would not look beyond the curtain of hair that hid me like an animal.

What happened? I was young and foolish, passionate, irrational, and immature. Many times in my childhood a path of love and learning ended abruptly due to a change in my family. We moved away from the people and the places I loved, and my learning and my talents suffered. I was very angry about it. In my adult life I ended relationships just when they became most important to others. I am afraid that no relationship will ever last for me, and that it is much too dangerous to share my life with anyone.

The archetypal Fool does not stay a fool however, he buries his dog and repents that in his wild rage he killed his own best friend. It is a time of atonement and forgiveness that transforms the Fool into a valiant warrior, who is now able to use moderating wisdom.

I need to make peace with those who seem to have wronged me. I can as a grown up choose not to disrupt relationships that bring me love, joy, progress, and growth. I can nurture everything I do with lifelong intentions if I want to.

As I sit here healing, I am grateful for my daughters because I know that even without being present, they receive my healing energies as I am healed. I know that love is a healing flow between us and that good news belongs to all of us.

This is the new road, the place of departure and the way for my advancement. A horse is waiting for me here. My highest aspirations in love, in spiritual growth, and in my occupation are fully supported by: two pages, two knights, a king, eight gold pieces, a lion, a very large tree, a goddess of mercy, and a super-bad spirit guide. I will be a fool no more. I have many friends.

6

What better method than questioning for discovery? Yet so many questions are rhetorical, and serve simply to express doubt. It may also be wisdom that comes back with a question, and wisdom is often painfully gained. It is not the goal of this book to increase pain so; I suggest if you must doubt and question everything, even the ground you stand upon, then why not try laying your question out as a statement? What good will that be? What good that will be.

On the other hand, ask and you shall receive. Ask: What is going on? Observe how you feel. Ask why. Listen. Follow the question and answer session till the end. Be gentle. Trust that the conversation leads to a compassionate place. Act on the power of your intuitive knowledge. Don't be afraid to do the math.

Being in love:
Something that either never or always works out.
Not being in love
Having a chance to make it work.
Being in love
Not being responsible for the outcome.
Not being in love
Being uncertain about the most important thing.
Being in love
Having an excuse for something you're not sure is wise.
Not being in love
Lacking confidence in yourself and others.
Being in love
Giving up doubts.

Not being in love
Using doubts to refine the deal, or
to carelessly clutter the table.

I'm going with involvement, and I'm not going to worry about, "Being in love" and what it means as long as we keep on rolling.

Piano Lessons

Piano lessons were my first clear failure - there had been no clear successes. My piano teacher recommended that I quit. My mother told me this and asked if I still wanted to continue. I said, "No." I had enjoyed piano lessons with previous teachers. Though it was not playing the piano that I remember liking most. I enjoyed waiting for the lesson in a half-imagined garden. This new teacher annoyed me with his metronome, and pushed my fingers around on the keys. He was reputed to be a very good teacher. My fingers didn't do anything right. My sisters were both excelling under his tutelage. My older sister was learning Ragtime and Billy Joel songs, she also sang along as she played. My younger sister made up songs on the piano. She was even more infuriatingly creative. I had to drop piano.

The piano was not the most beautiful instrument anyway; it was like a typewriter, mechanical, and completely un-portable. Imagine, hammers hitting strings! Compare it to the cello, the clarinet, or even a guitar…why would anyone play a piano? I was never sure why I didn't play it, because I couldn't? Because I hated it? Because my sisters played it better and learned it faster? Or because I didn't like my teacher?

With my new hobby, swing dancing, failure and success are far at the periphery, out of focus, edges to be avoided (blindly). I just like to keep dancing. I'm not interested in getting to know people, talking to them, or being friendly, though I wish people were more friendly with me, and I feel more comfortable dancing with people I know, or like, or who are friendly to me. I feel uncomfortable if a man starts talking to me and asking many questions and does not just use me for a dance partner, the way I am wanting to keep dancing with someone, anyone, not caring who. Sometimes it seems the better dancers do not ask me to dance. I make eye contact, even softly say the words "Want to dance?" but they walk on by. I must not be a good dancer, or a very nice person. I don't care.

Luckily I have a boyfriend who will dance with me most of the time, so that even if nobody else is dancing with me, he will keep me moving. Even if I never get good at dancing, I enjoy it. I decided to. Even if I have no feeling for the music, even if I cannot keep in step, even if I am not athletic, there is something I like about dancing. Perhaps it is the mindlessness, the proximity to others, the constant motion, the feeling of warmth and exhaustion.

I suppose expecting too much of yourself and comparing yourself to others does not help you to master something new. On top of that I do not have any natural talent for dance. I am shy, and don't pay much attention to others, don't like looking them in the eye and smiling, or going where they guide my body to go. I am not used to coordinating with others. It is hard for me to learn new steps; it is hard for me to ingrain what I learn. I have a body that looks like it would be good for dancing, people have often asked me if I was a dancer, and I was always sorry I was not. I am flexible, light, quick, and even graceful, but all this does not add up to being a good dancer. Perhaps if I keep at it, in five years I really will be good. Even if I am not, even If I'm really not that good, and still not even a very nice person, I hope someone will dance with me and keep me moving. I would have to be feeling sorry for myself to think that no one would dance with me, there is always someone who will, so I will keep on dancing.

Once upon a time a stained-glass artist was building his house near where I lived. I admired a guitar he had decorating a wall within his newly built home. He said it was handcrafted in Hawaii, that it had belonged to an old girlfriend who left it with him years ago. It was not in very good shape, but he said, "You should borrow it while I borrow your book of Gauguin paintings." So I agreed. I was working on an organic farm that summer, and one of the other workers played the guitar and gave lessons. I took a few lessons from him. I had too little money to take more. I had my children's education to put first. I had college loans hanging over my head. I didn't have a real job. I bartered for those three lessons with fortune cookies that were my little start up of a business. I'm not sure my teacher ever took the cookies though, and that bothered me. So I quit after three lessons. I was doing well for those few weeks. I practiced often. My teacher said I was learning fast and I felt sort of addicted to practicing. Until it got too hard. It got too hard when I decided I liked the Spanish style and wanted to play that way, not strumming chords but picking them rhythmically like a harp. When I loaded up my car and moved away, I returned the guitar, exchanging it for my Gauguin book. The car filled with my things caught fire, the Gauguin book was charred but the guitar was saved. Some years later, just last week, I bought a CD called simply Spanish Guitar music, and I began to want to hold that wooden craft of love and to stroke its sounds out.

When I first went to college I was wowed by the catalogue and decided to change my major from visual art to philosophy, but a friend of my previously unknown grandmother advised against it saying that philosophy is very hard and I would probably fail. I never took French in high school for the same reason. Everyone said French was much harder than Spanish. So I took Spanish. I didn't learn a thing. I don't know why the Spanish didn't take. Was it because my teacher was like one of the kids going partying and I didn't like to party? Was it because my sister was good at Spanish? Because I really wanted to take

French? Maybe I just wasn't good at languages? Maybe it was because I always forgot to bring my books home from school. I had taken a vow of silence. It was a secret vow so I had to talk sometimes or I would be forced to explain.

I still dream that someday I will learn to speak French, and Spanish too. Someday when I have the time and money to devote to this learning. Then I will feel very smart. I think that the definition of smart is to know more than one language. I like English a lot. It is hard to take in other languages when you like your own so much.

I love to learn things, but I forget most of them. Despite my random research and my abundant experience I claim to be an expert on nothing. None of it is rocket science; amateurs hold the key to everything that can be done. You don't have to be an expert to do anything or to accomplish something. To be an amateur seems more purposeful than to be an expert. Amateurs are need driven, experts are information driven. An expert is a commodity, an amateur is an adventurer. An expert creates an appearance, an amateur creates disappearance. I cannot seem to let go of my identity as an amateur, or to trade it in for the more socially valued expert identity. I wish that everyone else could see that knowledge does not belong to anyone, that it cannot be possessed, that there is value in just letting it float around unclaimed.

Why? Can it be that I am wrong? That I should claim, and account for all my intellectual property, should I define the width and depth of my knowledge instead of promoting my value as a know nothing?

Sometimes the greatest moment of learning for me is when I find out what I really believe and think, "Maybe I am wrong." Then take the other path.

Maybe we should just be friends. After the dance, you can still spend the night. I have been sleeping in the single bed lately, by the fireplace. You can have the bedroom. You could get me started in beekeeping, that way I will have gained something that is of lasting value. All I can think of is that you are not in love with me, and so the lump in my throat rises, and I do not see how we can be lovers if your feelings fall short of it. Where I was vulnerable and tender, I'll be guarded and bitter. What good will that be?

If you are ever going to fall in love with me, although I don't see why one has to fall, but if you were going to fall in love with me, you could do that after knowing me as a friend, instead of a lover. You could fall in love with me, someone you just hang out with as a friend, anytime, if you felt like it. I'm open to that.

After the dance, you did not come home with me because you have to get to work early. I did not say or do anything while we were together to change anything. I did not retreat or push forward. You hugged me good-bye. I kissed you on the cheek involuntarily. Sadly realizing it was involuntary. You asked about spending the night tomorrow after the dance. I said yes. I said nothing about lets just be friends. I could not turn you away. I don't know what will happen when you do come to spend the night. Sadly I think I will take whatever you will give me, I might even find myself giving something to you.

I feel so unsettled since you told me you felt uncertain about us for the long term, since you said you were not "in love." I struggle to stay focused on the little details of my life, the things I need to do, I am very distracted by this "something wrong" that I feel. I just watch the wheels spin anxiously. I fill my head with happy songs, I sing and hum, I think about my next dance class, my next writing class, when my beekeeping supplies will arrive and I can hammer together the bee boxes.

7

The meal, during a time of crisis or even when mildly anxious, can be hard to obtain with satisfaction. Yet food is the foundation of wellness and communion. You may find yourself unwilling to cook, and loathe to eat among others. You may be forced to find a source of reliable take out dinners, lunches, and snacks. You may find only bowls of kibble pleasing. Bored people like to munch. Maybe you are lazy, if so a liquid diet is for you.

Without food you wouldn't be alive. If you are alive you are male or female. If you suspend food consumption and take a step away from being alive, the next most basic question, "Male or female?" also becomes questionable, something to think about and decide.

O.K. Dudes ...Fasting

O.k. Dudes, I'm fasting today. It is 9:20 and I've only had tea. I cheated and added milk to the tea, local organic milk. I am not fasting to lose weight. I'm not fasting to detoxify my system. I'm not fasting to get closer to god. I'm fasting because I'm a copycat. When I like someone I learn from them by doing what they do. My boyfriend is fasting because he believes it's healthful. He does it once a year. I think it might be healthy, and I also think there may be a spiritual benefit. A utilitarian ethicist on National Public Radio said what we eat is really a bigger moral issue than sex.

I like to use the word "dudes", even though I know it is inappropriate. I call my daughters dudes, and then correct myself, "dudettes". I really like my daughters, so I imitate them. This has meant that as they reached adolescence I tried new, more feminine things. I got my ears pierced after both daughters had pierced theirs and the younger one even had double piercing in each ear. I bought myself some jewelry; I had never worn jewelry before. I started carrying a purse. I bought lipstick. I started shaving my legs and wearing a bra. I shaved under my armpits too. My younger daughter didn't know she was pretty until another girl in 6th grade told her she was the prettiest girl at school. Years later she told me that she met a guy who said he had known her mother in college. He told her she looked like her mother, and that her mother was a beautiful woman. I didn't know I was beautiful in college. I used to wear loose bright colored clothes back then. I didn't wear knits. I often wore a yellow lab coat, cinched around the waist. The person most similar to me in dress was an African student who stared at me in the post office. I stared at him too. More recently my older daughter told me she doesn't like it when I wear mannish shirts. She suggested I grow my hair out before I get old, kind of a last hurrah for feminine beauty. I have unexpectedly enjoyed trying these things so late in life. I have no interest in having my nails painted. I don't think lipstick looks good on me, so I stopped wearing it. Lip balm is fun though. I no longer wear jewelry, except an amber necklace that I like to rub my thumb on, and little diamond studs my boyfriend gave me. I have hardly worn earrings since I got my ears pierced. I tried for a while but the habit just didn't take. However I do wear the earrings my boyfriend gave me, they are the only ones I ever wear. Right now I'm wearing a new sweater he gave me. The sweater I am wearing now could easily be his, he may have bought it for himself and decided it didn't look right. It's a little mannish. When I like something I wear it all the time.

    Once visiting Ellis Island a museum guide referred to me as sir. I had short hair and was wearing a suit jacket. I was with my sister in law at the time. She was wearing lipstick and carrying a purse

    I have always had a hard time telling my left from my right. My mother taught me when I was young to pretend I was signing my name, and I would know by that feeling which way was right. I still have this habit of searching for direction by reaching for an imaginary pen. Sometimes when I'm driving I have to kind of shake my right hand to search for the right feeling, but often my right hand does not give me a clear signal that it is the right hand. I feel it could just as easily be my other hand reaching for the imaginary pen. I realized recently that the hand that is searching for the feeling of rightness is the right hand.

When a couple walks together it's proper etiquette, my boyfriend told me, for the man to walk on the outside and the woman to walk on the inside away from the cars. We were in NYC last weekend. I tried it, staying on the inside. I try to let him open doors, but not wanting to look like I'm trying I sometimes open doors for him, if it seems I'm by the door first. I'm a gentlewoman. When we dance sometimes I forget that I am the follower. "I can follow too" he told me once, and I was grateful.

I always felt lucky to have a woman's body. When I first got it I was about 14. I felt sorry for men that they don't have one.

Right now at 10:46 a.m. my fast is really beginning because I am getting hungry but I am not eating. As a small woman I have felt small and insignificant all my life. I like feeling kind of large as I stand next to my small man. I think there is a spirit that feels protective and wants to be formidable enough to protect loved ones who are often smaller and cuter.

He called and told me, "I really like you, you're a little different, and I like that, I'm a little different too."

"You're a little different? That's good, I like that too."

"I don't know if it's good it just is."

O.k. dudes, it's 2:37 p.m. and I've been hungry for a while. My thoughts turn toward the support of food but it's not there. When that happens I cut open a lemon, and put the juice in a glass with some maple syrup and water. I keep drinking that. The members of my Memoir and

Autobiography class are the dudes I am talking to here in my head. We have been reading She's Not There, A Life In Two Genders by Jennifer Finney Boylan. In a way this is my response paper. I'm two pages away from the end of the book

I learned two interesting things from She's Not There: Testosterone buffers men from the world. Estrogen makes your hair fluffy. Also I like the way she mentions all the times she or he was ignored, but she just goes on ignoring being ignored.

I just finished the book. My teacher, N., read it four times. When she told us that, I thought, well I'll never teach a writing class, because I only read books once. Having just finished the book I'm thinking maybe I could read it again.

I think I'm going to make it through this day of fasting. I'm not sure about the next day though. I'm really going to miss our classes, there are only three left. I loved reading and talking with you dudes and I even know your names G., M., J., and F.. It's a rare and wonderful thing for me to have such a handle on the situation. Mostly I glide through life blindly forgetting it as one forgets dreams.

New day, 8:19 a.m.: I am definitely feeling weak. Again I put milk in my tea this morning, two mugs. Now I am going do an inventory of the things I've done and thought about during my fast:

Cleaned the tub and shower

Cleaned the inside of my car

Just before the fast I did some mending of old jackets and finished nailing together my bee boxes, I feel like these two things should count even though the fast had not started officially yet.

I kept a fire going in the wood stove.

I got all my writings with N.'s comments on them together, in preparation for taking on the task of revising these pieces of work. They are in a stack, right here waiting. I finished She's Not There.

I've been researching tipis, wigwams and local

traditional Abenaki dwellings. I've been reading about how bees survive in the winter.

I called my mom and dad, and my two daughters.

I called my boyfriend with a question about painting the bee boxes, which was the last thing on my "to-do" list. I already had the paint out and was painting the first box. He said I should get some ventilation going if I was painting inside and that it might be better to wait for a warmer day and paint them outside. Then he yawned and suddenly I felt very sleepy. I realized he was right and put the lid back on the paint. We talked awhile longer. He was on the second day of his fast and the conversation was slow, as if under water. Long silences through which small phrases drifted, like pieces of seaweed I'd reach out slowly to touch. I opened the doors and let the fumes out, I told him I was going to take a nap and save painting for another day. Slowly we exchanged phrases like, thanks for calling, it was nice to talk to you, well, good-bye, talk to you later. I hung up and got into bed. My heart was beating faster, should I have said anything more? I put my arms around myself and went to sleep.

I've been thinking a lot about selling my house, paying off my debts, living in a tipi or wigwam, living very close to my boyfriend, building a house together, etc. But my house is so great, it is so comforting to lean on it when I am weak, everything I need is here. Hot water, electricity, my bed, my refrigerator, all my stuff. I camp out every summer, and it's always sweet to move back into my humble home. In addition, it's great to have a place where friends and family can visit. I wouldn't be thinking of moving, except that I want to be a lot closer to my boyfriend.

I've also been thinking about the book, <u>She's Not There</u>. I guess in the latest years of my life, so far, I've been coming out as a sexual person, whatever kind of sexual person I am as I figure that out, and yes, sort of decide it. It is a long and winding path. I feel more comfortable with it now that I'm in my forties. Also now they seem to make clothes for grown ups that are my size. Recently I bought a knit dress that fits so snugly that I decided not to wear it. I couldn't help buying it because I had never had the opportunity to buy anything that made me so shockingly visible. I guess I'm finding myself! Ha! That's funny.

I remember my junior high Home Economics class. There was a changing room with a three-way mirror so you could see your behind. I was shocked, "That can't be me! My butt can't be that big!" I was a skinny girl, and from the front I never knew how my hips just expanded back there. Oh yes another girl in the dressing room confirmed, "That's how you look, it really is that big." She drew my form in the air with her hands. Walking home from school, a car whizzes by and someone inside is shouting, "Nice ass!" I'm horrified

I am a very curious person. I'm not greedy. Being curious can lead to the same result as being greedy, especially for a forgetful person. I was thinking the other day that wedding rings are a good idea, because they serve as a reminder in case you get yourself into a tight spot. When I am dancing with someone I notice the feel of a wedding ring. It just pops out; it's a very clear signal. My first husband and I exchanged rings from a vending machine, they only lasted the day. My second husband and I exchanged real wedding rings, but mine was too big so I wore it on my middle finger, he did the same. This might not have been a clear sign of intention to me or anyone else. I think it would be very weak and stupid to suggest that a wedding ring worn on the right finger would make a person more faithful. Hey, sometimes silly things work, like my "to-do" lists. I always do the things on my list. I have ways of guiding myself to do what I want to do, what I intend to do, sometimes these little tricks help.

I don't want to stop fasting. I feel like someone in a Marc Chagall painting just floating above it all. I'm more aware of the other things I depend on like shelter, warmth, rest, and this sweet lemon water.

1:03 p.m., three minutes after lying down for a nap, after spending the noon hour sitting by the fire looking at pictures in Hands on the Land, I started to realize I was feeling very strange, perhaps too strange. I got up. I could hardly walk to the kitchen. I had a strange feeling in my head and legs, a blank weightless buzzing feeling. Buzzing is not exactly the right word; it was sort of like static, or a river roaring. Anyway I made it to the kitchen and cut open an orange. I juiced it and drank straight from the whatever you call it. I felt immediately revived and repeated the process, this time pouring it into a glass. Well, I'm glad I was home to get myself the orange juice.

Since I was fourteen I had heard that Indians could just die if they wanted to. I have always wanted to know that I too could just wish for death and get it if that's what I decided. I don't like the idea of life being involuntary, or having to resort to violence to end my own.

It was never my intention when I started this fast to begin dying. Now I feel chills. I put a sweater on and two more logs on the fire. It is pleasant to float above it all and to be uninvolved in this world, it is peaceful, it is unburdening. I'm not sure if my body needed cleansing, or if anything healthful happened. I think I do have a choice about being alive or dead. At this time I feel I have what it takes to live my life, so when the twilight comes, I just turn on the light.

When you are looking for something, searching and seeking for something you desire, feelings of uncertainty come up. You will have to navigate these ambiguities and choose to accept, refuse, or make an offer. Once you get yourself in a situation, and if you are seeking you must get yourself in situations, decisive use of the three basic gestures of accepting, refusing and offering must be accomplished. Yet before a decisive gesture can be made you must dig for some indication in yourself of what your feelings are saying. When you find something in your inner world, and if you dig you will find something, you may be able to decipher it and phrase it into a straight or hybrid version of yes, no, or maybe.

Summer

There is no way I could not feel the impact and the strangeness of every object in this house. I am staying at my boyfriend's house for a couple of weeks. I've sort of moved in. My things are in boxes on his exercise machine, and one drawer he cleared for me. In the summer I rent out my home on Lake Champlain, and this summer instead of camping in a tent, I'm living here. He has photos of his mother on the wall; she passed "into spirit" a few years before I met my boyfriend. I would rather call him my husband, but I would not tell him so to his face. Maybe two days from now I will tell him, and he will pull out a gun and shoot me. No, he is really very considerate. Nonetheless I am afraid to mention it. I don't want to appear insecure. He is really easy going. I would tell you how, in exactly what way he is so nice, but a fly has come from out of nowhere and is buzzing about the room, so I cannot tell you what makes him so fine, not with this distraction. Just now something happened, a very loud noise like thunder, perhaps it was thunder, and the fly landed on the window, so I leapt up with a book and whammy; the fly is smashed on the backside of my book. As I swatted the fly, I had not put down my cup of tea and a bit of hot water spilled onto the white blooms of an African violet. As I swatted the fly I also saw that during the act a hair of mine had fallen on the plant. I picked up the long brown hair and let it fall behind the furniture. I am conscious of my every move. Earlier I dusted all the furniture. It was very dusty. I had to pick up each of his things one by one. It occurred to me that this was very intimate, but that since I also make extra money by cleaning houses, I have done this very intimate thing for others, but it is not the same. Any one of these objects might hold some secret about him that I need to know. I dusted a picture that was on the floor, turned the other way. It was a picture cut from a magazine, a woman standing without clothes facing away from us showing her beautiful buttocks off against a dry landscape of cracked mud and empty sky. I dusted another picture, a watercolor of an Iris, displayed shrine-like with incense; on the back is a note from his previous girlfriend. I don't see anything of myself in this house. No, that's not true there is one thing, on the fridge, a rubbing of the frost on my window that I made and gave to him on our second date. There is nothing sentimental written on it. I am not a very sentimental person. I just say I love you a lot. This morning before he left for work, there was a moment we sat on the couch and as he held me I thought, "How wonderful this feels, how much I just want this moment." I thought to myself before I came to stay here, "I want to make it so he will never want me to leave." It is very quiet here now that the fly is gone.

    I just made dinner for us and it is all done. I'm starting to feel less surrounded by thorn bushes because a spicy meal is ready and soon I will not be alone in his house, observing it like an anthropologist, restraining the urge to tear things apart scientifically. Soon he will be here with me and we will be us and I won't notice the stranger all around me. My stranger. If he is strange, can he be mine?

I could start over. The beginning could be this toast I have buttered. Unable to move forward I could simply repeat the beginning. Slice the bread, put it in the toaster, and wait for the ding of the toaster-oven that tells of doneness. Butter the toast. Cut off any burnt edges eat the toast. If my narrative does not continue from this, I could repeat the process over and over until toast has nothing more to say, and in the toastless void the story would come. I have already had two pieces of toast just this way. The bread is dry, rather hard. The knife is large, heavy, and cuts very well through the stiff even sponge. I will go carve another piece, there is no sense saving a heel. Soon the toaster will ding, I am waiting. Upstairs someone is playing music that I am not enjoying. There are drums that remind me of an extra large facet dripping, also a stirring of an unknowable pot, somehow menacing. The toaster has dinged. I will spread the butter now. The toast is very soothing, though I am not particularly hungry. It's warmth in my hand and then in my mouth, along with it's gentle scratching of my tongue and throat are exquisitely familiar. I will have another. It is rather chilly in here although it is sunny and warm outside. Perhaps I should just lie out there soaking the sun up; perhaps I should toast myself. I went for a walk earlier today as is my custom and it was pleasant. The toaster dings. After this piece of toast warms and scratches me, something begins to happen that I have hardly noticed. The bread is sticking to my ribs. After this last piece of toast, a rounded nub, the heel of the heel, I will inevitably go for another walk. When I walk I think of nothing. I smell the wind. For a moment I absorb this, and then I walk on.

I traveled with my family to Avignon France earlier this summer. We stayed a week. Travel abroad has become a tradition, since the Paris trip. I think I started it. Whenever I begin to feel bleak and bored I believe it will cheer me up to get away, far away, to another country. My mother S. shares this love of travel, and maybe the idea that getting away is a good solution. All of my family lives far apart. Even my daughters now live in a different state. My daughters took French and Spanish classes at school. They also love to travel. I first planted the idea of going to Paris to cure the blahs in my mother's ear one dreary winter. My graduate school was doing a workshop in Paris, and sent me a post card. I called my mother on a day of dirty snow in Vermont. My mother flat in Kansas found an excuse for the trip right away. It would be a good high school graduation present for my eldest daughter, A.. It would be a good way for us all to be together. My mother doesn't like to compete with her grandchildren's social life… better to get away from it all. So that was the first trip, to Paris. The next year my sister's daughter graduated and they all went to Spain. This year T., my youngest daughter graduated, so we all went to Avignon France. It was T.'s choice, to go to France again, she wanted to practice her French. She also had a strong culinary interest.

  From a dream I woke with a silver cup in my hands, was it really mine? I doubted it, and I left it in the dream. Was that my silverware inside the cup? I doubted it and left those too as they were. These trips we take seem all about feeling my place within family. What part do I play?

  Somehow this group consisting of my eighteen-year-old daughter, my twenty-one year old daughter and my parents feels so comfortable, so much more comfortable than twenty-five years ago when my position in my family was "middle child". Now I feel like I have a place as securely as an old tree. Yet this security seems new to me and alien. I am not used to the feeling that I'm a valuable member of any group. I was not even sure I could find my way back to the inn. One night the girls decided to check and asked me to lead them home. I didn't know if I knew the way home, but I went the way that seemed right to me and found that I did know my way home.

A red rainbow appears in my dream as S. hangs his shirt up to dry, it is night and lightly raining. "There will be sun later," I say. I wonder if a red rainbow is still a rainbow and what it portends. "How afraid I am that this love will shift and I will ripple out of its folds."

Do I have to explain everything, even the presence of a pink ball of fuzz? Today is Sunday, yet I feel like I am supposed to accomplish something. At once I feel the need to shed ambition and am ashamed of my lack of ambition. Who rules ambition? Its force seems to come from cultural conditioning. The idea of ambition is warped. Warped by ideas of what you should do on Sunday. As if Sunday could divide leisure from one's occupational fate. Then there is the feeling of potential, and this too is ambition. It is a sort of wellness that is eager to apply itself to further feelings of possibility.

I had a nightmare last night that broke with words unable to be spoken, the empty speech-bubbles blurped into the oxygen of waking life. Disturbed by the effort to speak the dream scene warbled away. I remember broken pieces of a chair and trying to say, "Well it was fun for a while."

The last piece of visual art I created was made before I started seeing S.. It is a painted paper collage of a male nude on the beach. Should I tell S. about this man I knew? I got an email from him a few days back. He said he was sorry about how things ended between us and that he was thinking of me. He hoped to hear from me. I did not know him long; I spent only a long weekend with him. I had a great time on the weekend but later figured out that he was not a particularly good man. What haunted me for a while was wondering just how bad a man he might be. I chose him from photos on an Internet dating site. Can you choose someone based just on a photo? I decided to try. So I hopped in my car and drove to a strange city and ran up five flights of stairs to his apartment. I was nude within fifteen minutes. I had never made a drive by myself to a big city before. I was very proud that I had accomplished this without any problem. We went to the beach. I had a wonderful time at the beach, letting the salty waves lick me and wash me to the shore. He wandered off with his cell phone; he was in trouble with his last girlfriend. They were engaged, but he called it off at the last minute, because he fell in love with another old girlfriend. He and that old girlfriend did not stick together either, so sometimes she called too. When he returned to our beach towel he explained his views on the war, Bush, and being a Republican. I only listened and tried to understand. I was not disturbed by his woman trouble, or his politics. I simply enjoyed the day, the ocean, and the sky. There was a patch of a rainbow in one cloud that I watched throughout the day. I got rather sunburned. He said he loved me and asked me to marry him. Of course that was ridiculous, after knowing me only two days and I said, "You can't ask me that now." Over the weekend he reported himself as an American Indian, a republican, supportive of the war, and Bush as president. I also deduced he was a playboy, a liar, and obsessed with his body. He asked me to marry him again the next day and I said, "O.k." "When?" he asked. "Sometime after you come visit me," I answered. "I would take good care of you." He said. He never came and visited me. We stayed in touch by phone after I went home. I was loyal to him for a month or so even though he was not around, and I was very proud of my loyalty since I worry that I am not really a very loyal person after two failed marriages. Then he stopped calling and would not return my calls or emails. I was so disturbed by his inattention that I called every hour from 10:00 a.m. one day till 10:00 a.m. the next. I left messages that were full of my tears. In the last phone call I said, "You said you would take good care of me, and you are not taking good care of me at all and I don't want any more of it." Then he deleted me as a friend on Myspace.com. I felt a great relief at that point, a great relief that it was over. No relationship to have anxiety over, no more worrying about whom I had gotten myself involved with. So a year later I get this email. I let it sit in my inbox for a few days wondering if I should say, "Thanks for the belated apology." I am always concerned about karma. If I don't respond to the apology am I producing bad karma? Today I deleted the email without responding. I decided when the relationship officially ended that the best way to deal with my fear that he might do some ill against me, was to not give him any further attention and therefore not to attract any attention from him. Before we met we exchanged nude photos over the Internet, this was my idea. I sent him more on his birthday. I know that seems extraordinarily stupid, but I was extremely trusting, and I enjoyed it. I thought I was really cute and liked the idea that someone else might think so too. I enjoyed the pure silliness of it, the boldness. Perhaps I was just curious to see what would happen next. All these things I was doing were not things I had ever done before, like Internet dating. I wasn't waiting for what I wanted. I was searching without apology. I asked him in my very last email to destroy the photos. It has haunted me that he may still have them. I still have mine of him, he only sent three whereas I sent three dozen. I keep his nude pictures as ammo against his ever using mine for ill. I used my photos of him for art, a collage I now call "Republican at the beach". I did an excellent job with my subject. He is smoking a cigar in the picture, he is tan with a big red penis. I gave the painting to my mother. I enjoyed my long weekend in the strange city. He was generous and showed me a good time. I still feel I came out o.k. in the deal, except that I got a really expensive speeding ticket on the way home.

    Last night S. told me how much he appreciated me, he had told me several times already. S. thanked me again for all my help and fell asleep. Then as he slipped away into sleep an urgent feeling came to me that I had to tell him how much I loved him, but I didn't have the right words, I was getting choked up, my eyes began to water, I could hardly speak, "It means a lot to me to be able to be helpful to you and to have you to love." I managed to say at some point. I read once of some culture in the National Geographic where red is the traditional color for brides because it symbolizes joy. I like that because I have already worn a white dress and a black dress.

9

Talking about your home really means talking about where you come from. This is easy if you come from the same TV show as everyone else, but if there is anything complicated, confusing, or ugly to explain it's easier not to. Easier, but not necessarily better. By not talking about your home, you may come to feel homeless. Your place in the world is not acknowledged unless you add your location to the communal map. It's a social thing sometimes avoided and sometimes nurtured, this retelling of where you come from.

Talking about where you come from really means talking about your childhood. There is no better place than childhood to gather fragments of desire. These fragments are the important pieces of your heart that you can always recreate yourself from. Things can happen that seem to separate you from your own history as a child but it's worth going through the rubble to find the first thrilling things you knew. Often we look back to find the origin of some problem, but that may just be an excuse for going back home and reconnecting to that history.

Mastery

To hell with the nuclear family, when Martin Luther King was shot, my family moved into a communal household, an organization called the Religious House. It had a fancier name, The Institute of Cultural Affairs, but no one used it.

"How old were you then?"

"Eight, why, why does it matter?"

I was expecting some sort of magic, like I had hired a detective to find out how I ended up here.

" When a trauma occurs a person can become stuck at that stage of development. Eight years old is the time for mastery, a time when most kids learn to ride their bikes."

I was teaching myself obscure things when I was eight. I taught myself how to wiggle my ears, and how to meditate like the Buddha. I thought it was important to ignore discomfort so that I could maintain the lotus position indefinitely. At night sitting in my bottom bunk, I would pry my legs into the pretzel position and I'd stay that way till I fell asleep.

Crying was not allowed. If I cried I would only be annoying my sisters sleeping near by who were trying to make the best of the situation. Crying would not make my parents decide to take us back to what my sisters and I had considered paradise, a little ranch house in Saint Bernard Parish. With grown up eyes we would see that this big house in New Orleans that we shared with other families who were trying to make the world a better place was the real paradise, or maybe the road to paradise in 1968. Not having grown up eyes, all I saw was some sort of exile from my childhood. The lotus position now feels perfectly natural. I imagined leaving my body and streaming like an archer's arrow toward a red dot. I was the archer, the arrow, and the dot. To this day I am yogi-limber because of this early training.

I taught myself to wiggle my ears because I had heard that some people could do it, and I noticed that I could not. This seemed mysterious to me, that there was a part of the body that some people could move and others could not. I wondered if it could be learned. I tried to find the muscles that moved the ear, but I could not see or feel them. If there were such muscles, they did not signal their existence to me. I kept concentrating on the areas around my ears trying to feel, trying to communicate with what was back there, calling out in my mind, "Wiggle-ear muscle, are you there? Are you there?" For a long time there was no answer. It may have been when I started trying to move one eyebrow up and down that by accident the area behind the ear was felt answering, "Hey, I'm here, sort of behind your ear, but also inside your ear." I still cannot move one eyebrow up at a time. They both go up. I decided that one eyebrow up just wasn't my style.

I taught myself to live off raw salted potatoes stolen from the cupboard under the counter. I also ate figs from a branch of the tree that I climbed to get on top of the garage. We lived in a strange place with other families. I had a bike, which I had asked for. There was nothing wrong with it, except that it was just a bike, in isolation, without the context of home and family. Maybe that's my fault, maybe I am easily disoriented, maybe a normal child would not have lost her sense of family belonging when we moved into the Ecumenical Institute in New Orleans. The bike was just what I asked for. It had a banana seat, a basket and tassels hanging from the handlebars. Now that I had a bike, and could ride it without training wheels, I could run away. I could bring potatoes with me and sneak back for figs now and then. No one noticed when I ran away, they were busy doing other things, or perhaps I was just that sort of child who does very unnoticeable things to get attention.

There was another house that was as big as ours but did not have a group of families living together in what we called The Religious House. I liked to walk there, and look at it. This other house seemed abandoned, but it had an iron gate around it. In my dreams I walked over there, away from the other families. If I had been a sleepwalker no one would have noticed anyway. Was I was a sleepwalker? I had vivid dreams of walking to real places. If my parents didn't notice my outings, I wouldn't call it neglectful. Stealth has always been a virtue of mine, quietude my companion. What did I give them to notice?

The Religious House was an organization officially

known in 1970 as The Ecumenical Institute several years later it became known as, The Institute of Cultural Affairs, a private not-for–profit organization promoting positive change in communities, organizations, and individual lives in the United States and around the world. The Institute's objective is to help people find their own solutions to problems and the means to implement those solutions.

    My parents were Presbyterians wanting to do good in a troubled world. My mother said that the people she met at The Institute of Cultural Affairs were head and shoulders above the rest. This was not a hippie commune, but was sort of a cross between hippies and conservatives. Where exactly did my parents stand on the issues? It seems so touchy that to this day I have not asked. Were they for or against the Vietnam war? I think they were against it, without protesting openly. What about racial issues? I know they were for equality and were not at all racist – but that some racism was embedded in our family – some opinions are better kept quiet, for fear of alienation. I know they were upset by Martin Luther King's death. I know they were upset about the war. I think they may have wanted to change the world, but they didn't want to throw everything out like the hippies. They still valued tradition, but how can you make a bad thing better without changing it? Different branches of the Institute of Cultural Affairs were linked across the country, like a kind of machine spitting people out in different places randomly. The families involved in the Institute of Cultural Affairs were assigned to live in different houses after a year or so. When children reached the age of twelve they were sent away from their families to a different house far away.

    In the first religious house my family shared we lived in two adjoining rooms, parents in one, kids in the other. Then we were assigned to another satellite community in a different city, to build the church of the future. Moving people around to different houses in the network was part of the creative process for finding a new world vision. In the next religious house all the children lived downstairs, eleven girls including my big sister and my little sister in one room together and one boy in his own room; the grown-ups lived upstairs.

One day, I went upstairs. There was an unwritten rule about not going upstairs - or so I thought. There were other scary adults up there besides my parents. Perhaps they were not scary, but all adults, all strangers were somewhat scary to me then. Still I was brave and curious. I didn't even know if my parents would be up there. What would they be doing? Would I be interrupting something? How would they feel about my visit?

When I got upstairs, there was a big empty room. I knew the door in the left corner led to my parents' room. It was closed. Something else caught my attention; there was another door, off its hinges, and leaning against the wall. How strange. What was it doing there? A door off its hinges seemed very strange to me. Ideas about maintenance, repair, house building, etc., were not in my head. In my head somehow the "door-ness" of the door was heightened by the fact that it was off its hinges like that, leaning against a wall. It seemed like a sacred thing, the god of doors. I wanted to pray to it, pray for the opening of doors.

I went to the door and laid my hands upon it. I'm not sure how this happened, but the door began to move, and its weight was upon me. I was underneath the door, holding it up; and I felt in imminent danger of being crushed. With all my strength I held the door up, not knowing how long I could do this, having no idea how to save myself, and being too ashamed to call out for help. I had done something wrong, gone where I was not invited, touched what was none of my business. Just as my eyes were bursting with sweat and worry, a grown up walked by and took the door off my up-stretched hands. Without a word, the door was back up against the wall and the grown up was gone.

I went and knocked on my parents' door. It was very quiet in there. There were no smiles. I asked how Charlie had been. They said he was sick and might die. Charlie was a guinea pig that I had gotten from Santa for Christmas, in a strange rare Christmas that could have been read as a good sign or a bad sign depending on how you looked at it. Traditionally we spent Christmas with extended family in Louisiana where generations of my family had lived and celebrated. This past Christmas we were in Kansas, where we had no family, or friends. On the bright side, there was Christmas. Our little family my parents and my sisters, were together. The other families in the religious house were gone, and we got great presents, like Charlie my guinea pig. My younger sister got a doll she really wanted, but I noticed that it was really one of our old dolls dressed up to be new. This did not bother me too much because my little sister was happy with the doll and dressing up an old doll to be new was one of my moms old tricks. It wasn't a new "Religious House" trick, it was part of the "Eckles" tradition. So there was something affirming about this Christmas even though it was sort of creepy to be in a strange place without grandparents.

    I wasn't allowed to keep Charlie downstairs where I slept. My parents said Charlie swallowed glass. Something so ridiculous, so unlikely, that I couldn't even question it. In my mind's eye the glass lay waiting in the hay, and the little animal, perhaps curious, decided to eat it. I did not even ask how the glass got there. I knew life was not fair, I learned about that at snack time when there weren't enough cookies for each child and the day's lesson was for the children to try to make things as fair as they could. We kids had to figure it out. I knew other children did not have enough to eat, I had seen a picture of skinny black children squatting in a circle, I had seen Picasso's *Guernica*. These images and questions were part of the education children received at The Institute of Cultural Affairs. It would be fair, I thought, if I suffered like all the other neglected people in this world.

    Maybe it's the little traumas, like getting the wind knocked out of you for the first time, and not processing it with anyone. I was a traumatically quiet child, but "quiet" was also a reaction, a withdrawal into safety from a crazy world. Back then I didn't mention things like the door falling on me to my parents; everything that happened to me was in my own private universe. I don't even know if my sisters ever came to visit our parents upstairs in the religious house. They didn't have the guinea pig as an excuse, and who would want to climb the stairs into the adult world? I don't remember what I said to the shrink just before he said, "And when did that happen?" suggesting that what ever it was had been a trauma. I know I was talking about this time when we were in the religious house, but I never thought of this time in my life as traumatic. I love the idea that there could be an explanation for my lack of mastery, but I think the explanation is not so much that there was any trauma, just that some cats stay up in the tree ignoring even the smell of tuna fish. Some cats are stubborn.

The Religious House in Wichita Kansas, what a mess it was. The girl's dorm smelled like urine, very badly. Some kids cried all night. We hated the ones that cried because it was hard enough to sleep with all those shadows that look like witches and boogiemen, figures in every draping cloth. I dreamed of a beautiful fountain and wet my bed. I was so sad to find the profundity of the fountain gone and in its place my wet bed, a room full of stinky wet beds, and weird kids I didn't even like. I cried louder, longer, and harder than I had since the initial protest to this new life. My mother came down and told me that if I kept crying like that it would make me sick.

My mother gave me a large canister of red cloth and a needle and thread to make things with. This reminded me of the old days when I had my own desk, and I was an artist, with stampers in every shape and a crayon melter. I applied the melted colors, all rich, full, and wet, with a Q-tip to construction paper. I signed them all: " to mom and dad, love Alice" I had crayons and watercolors. My desk had been made of a door, held up by two cardboard filing cabinets with pink and green drawers. The desk was mine.

It was not communal property like things in the Religious House.

I sewed and sewed. I sewed purses of every size and shape, just purse after purse. They were not functional, but simply an exhibit of variety. I brought them to school one day for show and tell. One boy was so impressed he brought in a book and gave it to me, a sewing book with lots of red things in it.

Perhaps the crying did make me sick, because after that I did not go back to school. I saw the most beautiful color in the toilet, like a sunset, so beautiful I called someone over to see it. My dad had caught hepatitis from eating raw oysters which is a normal thing to do in New Orleans but apparently dangerous in Kansas, and I caught the hepatitis from him. Then I was sent to the hospital for the rest of the school year. Once I got used to being woken up all the time for shots, and used to the idea that I had bugs in my blood, I became quite fond of my life at the hospital.

It was good. I was really special to be there, having my own room, sleeping peacefully, calling the nurse with a button whenever I wanted. The button was great. I was scared to push it at first. Perhaps it was only for emergencies. I soon learned that it really was a system of "ask and you shall receive." If only I had had the button sooner, a parent button. My parents visited me in the hospital, I didn't have to go upstairs where the grown-ups lived to see them anymore.

It would seem strange to say I was happy in the hospital, but the causes for my unhappiness were removed, allowing for the natural recuperation of spirits. I had my own room, it didn't smell of urine, and my parents visited. I rested. I called the nurse if I was bored, or lonely or scared, and simply said what kind of ice cream I wanted: chocolate, vanilla, or swirl. I ate the ice cream and went to sleep. The nurse never indicated that I should be more reserved about pushing the button. If she had even once given an exasperated sigh, I might have gone into a coma,

I imagine.

Every summer and most holidays my sisters and I stayed with our grandparents at the Louisiana Baptist Children's Home, where Mamma and Dado were house parents. I don't know if I was a regular sleepwalker, but once I did find myself coming back inside at night from a back door at the children's home, carrying my musical bunny that played Edelweiss. I remember the tiny frogs all over the road, how the fields called to me, how I wandered to the kitchen garden. I remember getting up in the night one Easter and sitting in the bathroom talking to a cricket, when the Easter bunny, a purple and white figure as tall as a man, stopped in the doorway and told me to go back to bed, so I did. I know I wasn't the only one who left at night, some girls liked to go to the boy's dorm. That, I knew, was very bad.

How many of those kids were orphans, and how many just came from unsuitable homes, I don't know. I was a little kid, but I considered these big girls to be my friends. You didn't ask about people's parents here. Except one night we were having sort of a slumber party, so I asked this girl, whom I considered to be my best friend in the world, about her parents. She said, "My mother was a lady of the night and my father is a hobo." I laughed and kept repeating the word hobo over and over, till I finally said, "What's a hobo?" She explained that a hobo was one of these guys who ties a handkerchief on the end of a stick with his lunch inside and follows the railroad. Well, that made sense to me, and as for a lady of the night that seemed obvious, someone who walks around in beautiful clothes at night. This special friend gave me a parting gift of a turtle when she moved away.

There are two other stories I remember from the children's home. One was a murder story. The other was my first kiss. All my other memories from the children's home are blissful, heavenly, and full of love, good food, and happy holidays

Telling the murder story:

Raining, drizzling, an awful day. The newspaper, the New York Sunday Times, is laid out in sections on the floor, un-collated, de-junked, and displayed for a potential reader walking by, who turns the radio up, then down, unable to listen, unable to read, unable to write. I frown, frown at everything, there is nothing to smile about, nothing that I am thinking about right now. "I would like to be chopping vegetables right now." I think, "To be executing some part of a plan, a future dinner."

Instead of making the kind of meal that requires chopping lovely vegetables and mixing marinades, I end up making fried chicken. The recipe is not at all meditative, I have to keep turning the chicken, and worrying about the hot oil suddenly catching fire or spattering me as I put the chicken in. Cold water and then butter I use to wash and sooth my oil-spattered arm, quickly, before it turns red. Why? Why fried chicken? I have never made it before, but it is the earliest recipe I ever asked for. Alice the cook at the Louisiana Baptist Children's Home knew how to make the best fried chicken, and she was the first colored person I had ever talked with as a girl. I would sit on the back porch and help Alice shell peas, crack pecans, or snap green beans. It was one such time that I asked Alice if she had any children. Alice, the cook, told me that she had had a son, but that she came home one day and found him cut into pieces and stuffed into a suitcase. "Where?" I asked. "In the closet." She replied.

Did I ask any more questions? No, I continued snapping beans, because I liked to be helpful. One cannot always respond to what grown-ups say. Anyway, you're not supposed to; children are to be seen, not heard. I was torn between believing the story and thinking that it was some sort of punishment for my question. Curiosity killed the cat. Alice generally kept to herself, but I thought that since we happened to share the same first name maybe we might also have some other kind of kinship, even though Alice the cook was black. I kept this story in my mind, I never told anyone. I never believed it was true, not fully, especially not as I got older. It was a crazy thing, couldn't be true.

In my thirties I began reading about the civil rights movement and that whole period. I found that similar stories existed and realized that perhaps Alice the cook was simply telling the truth, since I had asked.

Finally during a rare visit back south in my 30's I asked my grandmother, "Did our cook have a son who was cut up and put in a suitcase?"

"Yes," my grandmother said, "that happened, but she should not have told you that. She had eight other children who all went to college."

So that is the murder story. It never occurred to me till this moment that maybe I should have pursued justice. I wish it had occurred to me a long time ago, but I am sure it is too late for justice. I was never a big fan of justice anyway, because I figure you can't change what happened.

"Do you know what a French kiss is?"
"No."
"Do you want to try it?"
"O.K."
"Do you want to try it again?"
"No, it's hot in here. Lets get out of this closet."

That year the Children's Home had changed, and summers were different. My old friends were gone. I was attracted only to an older girl who was really good at Ping-Pong. She had black hair that she wore in a ponytail, and large breasts. I wanted to be her friend, so I tried visiting her room.

"Do you want to play hide and go seek?"
"Yes."

We hid in the closet. The softness was particularly unsettling. The big girl's song was playing, "Feelings, whoa, whoa, whoa feelings." After that I stayed clear of the big girl's doorway. I didn't tell anyone about it. The same thing happened to a cousin who told grandma, who told us grandchildren to stay away from that big girl's door. Later we learned the big girl was in trouble for "making love."

"You are telling me that you are up shit creek, as you have described it. Now what do you need help with?" The psychiatrist asked her.
She didn't know why she was there; her husband had been seeing this psychiatrist for a long time, so she thought she'd try it.
"I don't know" she answered "but I hear a little voice saying, 'Make decisions.'"
"I would trust the little voice," he said. "When you hear a little voice, listen very closely to it. Wisdom speaks very softly."

When the little girl in pink, on her bike talks to me, I feel like I finally have a friend, and I don't feel like a 40-year-old woman. I feel like I am seven years old and the girl on the pink bike is talking to me. When I ride my bike--and briefly I am riding in the middle of these kids riding their bikes--I feel like I am one of them, included, riding my bike with the other kids.
It is like a time warp I ride through on my bike: into the group of young riders and then out of it. "Bye!" the girl in pink calls. "Bye" I wave, not looking back.
"It's late" I think out loud to myself.
The children love me now, but when I was a child I spent my playtime alone; why could this moment not have happened then? When I was young, I collected certain types of pebbles, small and smooth ones, white and black ones. I put them in certain places that represented times in the future, a place on the path I had not gotten to yet. The pebbles contained things, thought powers that could unfold and be very interesting later, at a different point in time when I would find them. Why I thought about the future before I was old enough to know what the future was, who knows? I did not concern myself too much with the

present. I did not believe in the days of the week or the clock. I tried to argue away the teaching of time in kindergarten—"it was wrong"--but I did not win. I refused to master the clock, jumbled the days of the week, and resisted the order of the months. I decided to hide under the table with these little boys who had speckled teeth and would not listen to the teacher teaching how-to-tell-time for their own reasons.

Sometimes I imagine there is someone in the cosmos who never forgets. Sometimes I hear something beyond the crack in the eggshell, our sky, like wind blowing, whistling through that gap.

Something, not just time and how it should be told, but many things seemed wrong.

Today I take a sample of my hair and look at it closely. Things are not as they seem. It seemed that my hair was turning golden from the summer sun, but looking closely now, I can see many transparent strands. These strands, having no color, make my hair look lighter in general; they reflect the pale golden color, where they used to deepen the brown darkness of my hair. Taken singly; one can see, these are gray hairs. In any given section when I look closely at the mix, there are many of these hairs, the colorless ones. As long as some of my hairs have color, the others appear only to be a lighter shade, when in fact, they are gray. When I was young, I had this light golden brown hair, the lightest hair in the family; My sister said it was because I was adopted. Hair color is not solid, but a sort of elongated pointillism.

Children do not perceive dark brown, at least not in hair color. When I was young, many people had black hair. Anyone my age would agree, "Most grown-ups have black hair." Then one day I realized how few people actually have black hair. Kids argue about this, only the older ones believe that most grown-ups have brown hair, and not black. Younger children do not really perceive the darkest dark; perception of darkness drops off at dark brown. I've heard there was a time in history when people saw blue as black, their perception of darkness dropped off at dark blue, or maybe all blue. Blue is the beginning of darkness.

To change color is one thing, but to lose color - is that what is happening? Name a creature that is colorless? Jellyfish. Am I going to be like a jellyfish?

What am I going to be? What have I mastered? What was my trauma? Trauma was all around me; I didn't have to own it to stumble on it. I taught myself an odd collection of things, wiggling my ears, sitting in the lotus position, doing a cartwheel, sewing little red purses, all without notice. I didn't do any schoolwork in third grade, I was sick almost the whole year. When I got out of the hospital, the end-of-the-year-party-in-the-park was all that was left, but I did not find anyone I knew there. I ate a hot dog and left. Then we moved away.

I was wondering how to keep the air in my tires, metaphorically. It would help if I got some caps to cover the nozzles where the air gets pumped in. Yeah. I can't just be open all the time, letting what pumps me up seep away. You get your tires filled up, and then you put the caps on to keep the air in. That's how it works with other inflatables.

Finding one's place in the world is not always easy. Erik Erikson, 1902 -1994, was an artist, teacher and psychoanalyst. The development of identity was among his chief concerns. In 1972 and 1973 when much of this story takes place, I would have been, according to Erikson's <u>Theory of Psychosocial Development</u>, in the fourth stage, Industry vs. Inferiority, that occurs between six years and puberty. One of the great events of this time of life is the beginning of school. The child enters the larger world of knowledge and work. Not only at school but also at home, friends' houses, and on the street this learning occurs. According to Eriksons' theory, successful experiences give the child a feeling of competence and mastery, while failure gives the child a sense of inadequacy and inferiority. At my root I feel I know nothing. If I do master something, I don't believe it, or feel it is so trivial as not to be an accomplishment at all. Other things I reject before even trying. All this can lead to a feeling that one is a "good-for-nothing".

Everything I know is inside my mouth. These ridges are the mountains I have climbed, my philosopher's stone, and my primitive tools. I have never liked them. These bones stand uncomfortably like tombstones leaning this way and that. My smile is huge, exposing everything I have: the big front teeth, the pointy side ones, the ones that hide behind others shyly, and silver cavities glinting like ice in the mountains. I have never been able to smile without showing all this.

My jaw is imperfect. Since I noticed this as a teenager, I have always held my mouth in a way to compensate for my weak chin. It was a dead giveaway to how weak I was. I also changed my handwriting. I purposely crossed my "t's" with a long glide of my pencil to show determination.

Part of growing older is perfecting yourself. The other part is the fact that things are not going to get better so long as you are heading toward the grave, and what choice do you have? That is the direction time moves in, I think.

In a dream I took my teeth out, the ones on the upper right quadrant. I pulled them out one by one, complete with the roots. I cleaned them and hung them up to dry. Then I was going to put them back in so that they were straight. But I was afraid. I asked my daughter to help, but she thought it was ridiculous that she should help with such a thing. I knew it was. So I began sorting my teeth out. Trying to get them in the right order. I found it was not as hard as I thought it was going to be. There were symbols on the bottom of the teeth that helped me match them up with the ones on the other side. I put them back in their sockets one by one, and moved them around till they were straight and orderly. I had a large boney toothy structure left over that did not seem to fit in. It was like a dinosaur bone. I was sort of sad that the puzzle did not fit back together, but everything seemed so improved without that dinosaur bone in my mouth.

    J. F. Gauthier Elementary School in Saint Bernard Parish, New Orleans was integrated in the fall of 1960 under court order, ten years before I started going to school there. On the playground there were shouts of, "A fight, a fight, a nigger and a white". I spent recess far out in the field by myself looking for four leaf clovers. I found dozens of four-leaf clovers at the far end of the school grounds; I put them in a good luck bank, between the pages of <u>Ramona the Brave</u>. I didn't have any idea why there were fights, or why they were always between a black child and a white child, or why the teachers let them fight. All I knew is that it was scary. This was years before I read <u>Ramona the Brave</u>; I was just learning to read Dr. Seuss at the time. The teacher called us in from recess and I got hot running. I saw a black girl with her sweater tied around her waist. I thought that was such a smart and cool thing to do, that that's what I did too. When the teacher saw me, she put her hand on my shoulder and said, "Don't wear your sweater like that, that's how colored girls wear their sweaters". Later after we mover to Wichita, Kansas I thought, "It is unfair that I can't imitate black girls." There was a black girl in my class who could do all sorts of tumbling, besides just cartwheels. I wanted to learn to do everything she did. I tried to teach myself in private but never mastered a certain back flip.

10

Making excuses is painful, but if you think about it, it is the first step in acknowledging something that can no longer be denied. Even a devious naming of what is can be the beginning of acceptance and forgiveness of the way it is.

The very short essay that follows is an imaginary conversation addressing how I feel about a real history I share with a real friend.

The Race

"What do you want from me? After all I've done for you over the years, whenever you needed a little boost for your self esteem I gave it to you, and still you act like I'm your nemesis instead of your friend."

Before I answer, I want to tell you about the big one that got away. A little story singing, "Nanny nanny boo boo" was just to the side of my thinking about why I hold you in animosity despite our friendship. I saw the little vignette shining bright like the inside of a star far away. I could see it as if I were close up. The story bleeped to me from inside the star was part of a constellation of stars that together formed a creature answering "why". If the star had not faded, if it had shone a little longer illuminating the head or tail or what part I don't know of this creature I would have been able to identify the creature and perhaps had some idea "why".

Running, running we were running together in the same race, we started at the same time but for some reason you took off ahead of me leaving me in the dust. I was envious of your accolades. I could list my personal obstacles, and explain why I didn't win and why I have not arrived yet, I could line up my challenges next to yours. I could say I took time out to have children, or even simply I am a woman, but no explanation soothes the hurt proximity of our ambitions when we were in our 20's. My animosity is reserved for you because of this, the lost proximity of ambitions. We started in the same place, for a short time we had the same race ahead of us, how can I forgive you for that? I could be envious of other runners better than you, but you hold my 22 year old heart on the gold, you got the gold, and I run in the park.

     My friend offered that he wanted to bribe me out of my animosity, and I began to contemplate the bribes I might take. When I first discovered I had this animosity toward my friend I thought, "Well this is bad but I'll give it up when I'm ready." Suddenly I felt I could not wait one minute. So I made a counter offer, I'll forgive you the next time I see a Chickadee. I asked him to send a Chickadee for his bribe. Since I see this bird quite often anyway, it wasn't long before the deal was done. I am often reminded to forgive, and to enjoy friendship completely. The Chickadee is a very friendly bird and seems eager, like a dolphin, for play.

Part Three:
Living With Full Spectrum Communication

As I have been reaching the end of this project I have been realizing what it means to write *A Phrase Book for Spiritual Emergencies*. It means I have to heal myself and be a healer. I don't think of myself as one of those new age people who plasters their world with affirmations. I just wanted to be a great writer. My obstacle to finishing this book was how to organize it. Other writers helped me select the title and I decided to organize it around the title as if it were an actual phrase book, a self-help book for spiritual emergencies. I am familiar with that structure as I am always trying to teach myself something, a new language for instance. Other writers suggested that it could be a straight self-help book with some humor. I found myself constructing with my essays a new age self help book that hopefully could also be called literary. I have now plastered my world with affirmations. Why not? If so many people believe, "Being positive" works, and I have been meeting increasing numbers of these positive people, then I guess you can't fight the system, and the system is "super nice". On New Year's I wrote six word resolutions and cut and pasted them in various places around the house.

The mirror above my bureau:
"Be aware of hidden mission today"

A map of where I live:
" Believe you can and do magic"

My water purifier, near the spigot:
"Help yourself, and help someone else"

A windowsill:
"Save what you love, discard regrets"

A bookshelf near the door:
"Reduce expenses, work less, become famous"

The radio:
"Stay young, become wise, draw smiles"

Under glass on the coffee table:
"Read more, worry less, keep boyfriend"

    Today I printed up a bunch more, affirmations I picked out from Louise L. Hay's <u>You Can Heal Your Life</u> and I posted them in various places around the house. I enjoyed deciding where to put each one. Placing a phrase in your house may add another therapeutic touch to the process! "Still life with affirmations" I said to myself with a smile. As a visual artist this pleased me. It's so surreal I thought. I like the way objects, places, and dramatic context can increase the power of words by exercising their meanings in the practice of daily life. The home and the objects we see, touch, and use daily is a kind of mirror we walk through all the time.
    Louise Hay recommends saying affirmations to yourself in the mirror. I think that's good but the mirror is all around us, in our things, our lives, and our people. I like the idea of placing these affirmations where I will meet them and where you might need them on your path. Before placing an affirmation I would ask myself, "Where am I likely to be when I am thinking something opposite of the affirmation?" At what point on my path do I need to be reminded of this? What object in my house affirms the affirmation? What objects benefit from the affirmation? Those are the places I have posted them.

My calendar:
I am important. I count. I now care for and nourish myself with love and with joy. I allow others the freedom to be who they are. We are all safe and free.

My refrigerator:
I take in and give out nourishment in perfect balance.

The compost bucket:
I lovingly forgive and release all of the past. I choose to fill my world with joy. I love and approve of myself.

The potting container of my lemon tree plant:
I give myself permission to be all that I can be, and I deserve the very best in life. I love and appreciate myself and others.

The trash can:
I am willing to release the pattern in my consciousness that has created this condition.

The refrigerator:
I deserve the best and I accept it now.

The wall, in my writing room:
There is nobody like me. I am being myself. I'm doing this for the fun of it. There are people out there looking for exactly what I have to offer. I am letting them know I exist.

The front door:
I am willing to change. I am always Divinely protected and guided.

The wall, in my writing room:
I am making good money being a writer.

The mirror:
Alice you are wonderful, and I love you. This is one of the best days of your life. Everything is working out for your highest good. Whatever you need to know is revealed to you. Whatever you need comes to you.

    I sang and recorded that last one as my new ring tone. I started recording little ditties I made up for my ring tone a while back, sort of accidentally. I didn't want to forget a little song I made up while singing in the car so I took out the cell phone and used the record function. Then a prompt came up on the phone, "Use as ring tone?" I clicked yes and have been singing in public ever since. I decided it was a good practice to get used to hearing my voice, and self-expression out in the world. At first it was embarrassing but I got used to it. It is good to get used to being yourself in public. I've moved through several different ring tone songs by now, this affirmation ditty is the first that I didn't make up, although I suppose I did make up the tune, or maybe it is remembered from somewhere… We'll see how this one feels. In the past once I get used to hearing myself break out into song anytime any place, I feel good about not keeping myself a secret anymore.
    Long ago a friend mentioned Louise Hay to me suggesting maybe I was working along the same new age lines, but I thought that was silly at the time and I didn't want to know more. Though I never forgot her name. Recently I went to a health expo with my partner who wrote, <u>Natural Beekeeping</u>. He was giving a talk and I came along for fun. We visited a psychic and an aura photographer. I felt very open to what each had to say, the vibration seemed right, I felt in agreement. I have never gone to a psychic before, but impulsively I just did it. Among other things she briefly mentioned Hay's book. I went out and bought it the next week. The aura photographer asked if I did Reiki, I said no, and she said empathetically, "Why not?" She pointed out the teaching

and healing energies in my aura photograph. So I bought a book on Reiki. Later that day after buying the book I met a man who asked, "What was the Reiki book I saw you with before?" He had just been attuned, I had just learned from browsing the first part of the book what that meant. We talked for a while. I mentioned that the author of the book thought it was very important to pass the ability to do Reiki on, to teach others how. He said, "It's happening all the time." We parted shaking hands and I definitely saw in my mind a ball of light pass from him to me. I noticed that I was a little shy about taking the energy. I thought maybe I should get back to my students; I was with them on a field trip. I also knew they didn't need my supervision, they were college students. In my mind I saw our hand shake like white light pulsing toward me through my hand, up my arm, warming me. I felt it, slow, alive, grounding. The exhibit we were seeing was also very moving, Combat Paper. Veterans cut up their uniforms and made paper of it and expressed their feelings all over it with words images and sculpture. I dreamed that each step in the process of paper making was clearing or therapeutic in a different way.

11

Figuring out what's going on is one of the great opportunities of a spiritual or emotional emergency. It can be fun when things don't make the usual kind of sense to turn your picture upside down and see it a different way! If you like figuring things out start by playing with the puzzling pieces and before you know it you will have entertained yourself for hours. Who has an emergency now? The wisest thing is probably to let go of your obsessions, but if you must admit to being obsessed, use it. Obsession is art therapy. Use thoughts, words, phrases, and communication to explore what is obsessing you till you are pleased with the resulting manifestation. When you are pleased, you are appeased and able to let go of the thing that was bothering you. Art is a form of communication but not always a welcome form. Maybe what makes it art is persistence. Eventually, when the artist finds his or her necessity it will be recognized as a universal human need.

October, A Short Mystery

I am making my weekly schedule, and having a hard time fitting in things like "take a shower." I've allotted three hours each day to write. It would be great if I could sleep while I write. I made the schedule to prevent multitasking, so I would have a dedicated time slot for each thing. Now instead of multitasking there is multi-relaxing, a form of relaxing where something important must get done, for example showering, getting some exercise, having dinner, finishing the laundry. I really enjoyed my walk today, even though I was multi-relaxing, I was walking and reading a printed out email at the same time. I had my knee-high rubber boots on, a camel hair coat and cashmere scarf. It was practically raining. There was a heavy mist with droplets in it. My papers were almost getting wet; I rolled previous pages like a visor so that the rain stayed off the current page. Who would send me such a long email you might wonder. My daughter in Cuba. I walked along the beach reading of her times there. I love the feeling of being outdoors, even on inhospitable evenings like this. The water is low and the shore weaves in and out, I walk its curvy line. In and out I weave staying close to the water's edge. When I love this place, my house in North Hero on Lake Champlain, I worry about how I can be partners with a man in Middlebury, Vermont. Will I ever belong anyplace else? Can I belong more than one place? How? My daughter says in her email that she read my piece about fasting and couldn't stop laughing. I can't save the falling apart world; I just try to hold together my little life. I'm not trying to be funny; I'm just being honest about my shortcomings while sneaking in a few self-glorifying details. Now my hair is drying, I brushed it and a lot of hair came out. I've been losing loads of it, it seems. My hair is not visibly thinner. I think what is happening is that the hairs that fall out are being replaced with white hairs.

So I have been plowing through this book, <u>He Named the Streams Flowing Around Various Shaped Rocks</u>, chapter by chapter every night. My anger is dissolving like an Alka-Seltzer in a glass of water, just like on TV, but I am angry to lose my anger. The author of this book, Lee Who Stung, is not responding to my email in a way that satisfies me. I am reading the book of a person who rejected my friendship. When he writes of the misunderstood cold silent exterior of the Asian man, he cannot redeem this man for me, even though he is the hero, the main character of the story, I don't like him, because he doesn't like me. One likes to feel like they are friends with the author, even if it is fiction, one feels that the author is living through one of the main characters and so in a way, he is that character. If you know you are not friends with the author then the fantasy, or possibly, even the reality of a personal connection is lost. Therefore if you learn anything from the book it will not be by heart.

You have ignored me and I have ignored you back. I painted a picture of you ignoring me, and then took defensive action. I wish I could forgive myself as easily as a man forgives a pretty woman. I don't even know if that is a productive myth.

I just realized there is a hidden character in this story. A character that is right here in this story but the author is not telling you about him or her. I do not know exactly who the secret character is, at the same time I know I cannot trust you the reader with the character's identity. I don't know if it is a side to myself, a side of my life, or an edge I share with someone else. The character is secret from me. My dreams do not offer up a name for this presence. I don't know if I am keeping the secret from myself, or if I have just come to the limits of my perception.

It is dark and cold outside, and so cozy here in bed. Five minutes after the alarm went off I lay half asleep sorting out the tail ends of dreams:

"Can I leave my purse here, with all this money in it, right in the doorway where you are sitting?" I asked a character in my dreams.

"That depends on when you'll be back." She asked, "When will you be back?"

I thought about it and said, "Five o-clock"

"That's late" she said, "people will be coming in for the evening show, better take it with you."

So I grabbed my purse and some papers that were nearby for my research. Then the alarm went off and it was five o-clock, but it was not late, it was early.

My research reveals only empty coincidences. It would be impossible to make up stories if coincidences were not empty, and even after you fill them they have a way of emptying themselves again. I suspect I'm on both sides of this issue. I'm slightly more on my side, because I know my side best. The other side is my secret character's side.

A girl caught my eye; I saw that she was the age I once was. I realized that she had replaced me in that age.

What if my old selves did not disappear, what if it were possible that I might meet my former selves on the street, the college girl, the drop out, the pregnant girl, the young woman with small children, what if they all still existed?

Every specific detail I can dig up about myself is precious, every fact of my biography, the clothes I wore, the conversations I had, the places I lived, it all seems beautifully unique to me even though I have been replaced a thousand times. Everything I told Lee Who Stung about myself, those are really important things, the thread that sews my history together, and the flesh on the frame of my name. So I was angry that a character lacking my history, unable to compete with my memories was somehow beating me in a name game. It is ridiculous to compete with fictional characters, I suppose.

I am not embarrassed easily, but I do find my correspondence with Lee Who Stung embarrassing. I had no particular interest in him other than that he was an author who had used my name for a fictional character. Perhaps unknowingly? I hoped that my curiosity would be met with an equal curiosity. Forgetting the taboo against it all, man/woman, and celebrity/ordinary person.

Here is a series of emails with the subject heading: A short Mystery, and later, Jacket:

Dear None Of-

Do you know Lee Who Stung, author of He Named the Streams Flowing Around Various Shaped Rocks? I have not read the book, but apparently I am quoted in it.

"All thinking is wishful thinking," [Alice Eckles] might say, the words stirring mantra-like from her throat.... "
(p.197)

I was thinking for a long time that it must be some other "Alice Eckles". But now that my parents have bothered to send me this scholarly review of books concerning language for language sake, I am noticing several things. First, I am the same age as the author. Also, I did take remedial speech classes in 3rd grade. Also, race was an issue in my childhood - but why even if it was me- and we shared some part of childhood - would the author use my full name? It would be strange for him to even remember my name. Alice is described as very pale, as I was. She wore a sky blue button up sweater - I don't remember having or wearing a sky blue button up sweater. I did wear a pair of ultra marine overalls, frequently, with a pink elephant patch on the front (I liked patches). The elephant was not sewn on, but held on with a safety pin, so that it curled up and was not very visible. I don't know if Lee Who Stung realizes this, but I am the invisible one, and he is a famous author, writing about our inequity of visibility. I would like to talk to him if indeed I am Alice Eckles. I would like to tell him I was not making fun of him in remedial speech, and while he was trying to model his voice on my southern white babble (we had just moved from New Orleans to Wichita Kansas), I was secretly trying to do cartwheels modeled after a black girl in our class. But I spent most of that year in the hospital, doubling my invisibility.

(I sent this to None Of and pasted it into the email below that I sent to Lee Who Stung.)

Dear Lee Who Stung -
    Maybe this letter is premature before reading your book, but I'm eager to express my curiosity. I think that even if I am not the Alice Eckles in <u>He Named the Streams Flowing Around Various Shaped Rocks</u>; there are things I want to know. I have just now read the first few pages of your book on Amazon.com... They show the cover, and I notice; this is a novel, it's fiction. So Alice Eckles is just a

made up name? This has nothing to do with me, directly? I am a writer, and I am writing nonfiction about my life. So if we went to the same school, I'd like to talk with you about it, maybe. I cannot remember the other person in my speech therapy class. I thought they were trying to take the New Orleans mumble out of me. Please at least respond yes or no to the question, "Could I be the very same Alice Eckles referred to in <u>He Named the Streams Flowing Around Various Shaped Rocks</u>?

Thanks, Alice

New message:

Dear Alice,
      How sweet it is, to get a note from one of my female fabrications! Although the coincidences are remarkable, you appear in my novel the way people find pennies on the sidewalk, the name simply came to me in moment of inspiration! Hope this clears things up, and hope you enjoy the book.

Yours,
Lee Who Stung

New message:

Dear Lee Who Stung,
      My middle name is Lee, just to add to the coincidences. Being southern, as a child I was called Alice Lee (something I misunderstood for a long time). I have ordered your book. I was wondering if you could write a novel where you solve all my problems, and then I could read it and figure everything out. O.K. not all my problems just one. I was thinking of writing an open letter of crisis. The crisis is not at all imminent; it is about twenty years down the road (experts now say less). AE cannot solve her problem, but she goes on happily for many years

ignoring the problem. Her solution to the problem is that when the problem becomes too much of a problem she will die. Health will not be a problem for AE, by rights she could live to be 104. Levity is not a problem for AE by rights could stay in the air or at least above ground indefinitely. Money is the problem, when AE can no longer pay her bills she will off herself. Will she be a grandmother by that time? So far ignoring the problem works, life goes on, credit cards are approved, and it's a beautiful life, in spite of its unworkability. Like global warming, a problem ignored is such a huge bummer later on. AE would do something about the problem if she saw the solution to her problem, but not seeing a solution, with all her might, not being able to imagine, figure out, or even copy a workable financial plan for affording her life - she feels the best she can do is not worry about it too much and go on living. That doesn't mean she doesn't see what's coming. One of AE's characteristics is that she is uncompromising. She is not going to cave in and do what others do to survive, she does everything her way, because that's the way she likes it, and then there will be a final straw. When she is, say sixty, tired of teaching and cleaning houses. Perhaps it will be a heating expense, she may be tired of stacking wood. She knows how to freeze. Perhaps you might think her children would intervene, but they would never know, she seems capable and upbeat. Besides her debt to her family is so deep and sorrowful, the last thing she wants to do is add to it. What choice is there but to add to it? If she lives, someone else will have to pay her heating bill, etc., If she offs herself, she takes away some of what she was meant to give, to them. Is it so hard just to provide for oneself? It is a puzzle AE can't seem to solve to her satisfaction.

I want a story where crisis is averted. I don't know how to avert the crisis. I write nonfiction about the present day, in which there are no solutions for growing debt.

Another thing about AE, she is not a gambler. Yet, the typical artist/writer career is a gamble. Perhaps now we have all been relegated to gambling regardless of career. For AE a solution to money problems is not a solution unless it's a sure thing. People who know AE would not describe her as so cautious, not at all. It's not caution; it's laziness. AE does not want to exert energy with the intent on making money if the money is not a sure thing. She has talents that go wasted because she refuses to take a chance on wasting them. She drives a hard bargain. She will settle for nothing less, and thinks everyone else is stupid for doing so.

Thanks for your answer, and for being pleased to hear from me. Maybe you can recommend a story that would model for me how to avert such a crisis as I foresee.

AE

New message:

Lee Who Stung -
Do you think maybe you might have met me briefly in a friend's Brooklyn apartment say about 1986 and given me a tan jacket, because I said I liked it?
Was that an exchange, jacket for name?

Alice Eckles

New Message:

How peculiar, that rings so true to me. But if it happened at all, it was likely after 1987, '86 is out of the question.... Who are your friends and what exactly do you look like? Your story intrigues me....

LWS

New message:

LWS-

It couldn't have been after 87 because my daughter was born in 86. She was conceived in that apartment. My boyfriend Your Business and I were staying there in None Of's apartment. My hair is very straight and brown. My eyes are very blue and large. I may have read a short story I called Stable Rat. I was pale. I'm fair skinned, but have had more color in my cheeks since a trip to Spain during the first Gulf War. I'm petite, 5' 2". Didn't wear a bra back then. I was 20 but looked a lot younger probably. Here I'm falling into a trap of describing my looks to a strange man who gave his jacket away in the wrong year. This is for identification purposes only. I have a King Bee. Why did you use the word "exactly"? I could enjoy giving a long description of "what exactly I look like" But for identification purposes I don't know if most people notice I have crooked teeth. Even though I have a very large smile. It may have gotten larger over the years. Back then my cheeks were fatter. My chin is pointy; I have a triangle shaped face. Oh! - Instead of having long straight hair like I do now, back then I had short straight hair; it may have been standing straight up. I was only in Brooklyn a month; it was an odd slice of time, as most of my life is made up of very short eras. I tend to pretzel my body when sitting. My head is kind of small. I'm not zaftig - that would be chubby in a nice way - right? I remember that word from that era. Would your jacket have fit me? Because the jacket did fit. I don't have it anymore, though I did wear it for a few years.

    I believe we were talking about names that day. If so, what name was mentioned that was just too weird to be true and yet was felt as ordinary by the people who knew him? The initials are G.H. or maybe G.B. . Maybe your memory is better. If we ever met... If that was the conversation happening that day...If my memory corresponds to anyone else's anyway.

Alice Eckles

New message:

LWS-

    I think we can solve this whole thing by just being friends. Being friends would make it o.k. that you used my name. It would make it o.k. that I have sent the previous notes.

    If we were friends we would have to have an agreement of mutual non-interest in each other as anything more than friends. Of course I don't know you so my offer is premature - like using my name before you knew me.

    I'm still interested to know if we met and exchanged jacket for name. It is hard for me to believe in coincidence.

    I've read up to page 130 in *He Named the Streams Flowing Around Various Shaped Rocks*

    -AE

Draft email never sent:

Lee Who Stung -

    Please at least answer the question. I remember when (you?) gave me the jacket. There was absolutely no hesitation. I said I liked it, and you took it off and gave it to me. I didn't know what the gesture expressed, but here are a few ideas

    You thought I was stupid for liking the jacket. You were not attached to this sign of your ethnicity, and wanted to say so. You were generous. You wanted to give me something. You wanted to cover me up. You hated the jacket. You practiced non-attachment generally. You liked me

Did you like me? Friends like each other. We could be friends based on that. I liked you, and your jacket. Even though I didn't know you, I didn't know if you were kind, or if you were sneering at me.

    I guess the only thing for me to do is stop caring and write a book with your name in it, maybe the book were I let out all my beautiful anger. Maybe you will stand for all the isolation. The only thing is I write nonfiction, so all I can say is: He never answered. I don't know why you are not answering me. Yes or no, was it you? If you don't want to be friends, fine. If it wasn't you, I'm sorry for bothering you.

    Am I the only "Alice Eckles" who is so sensitive about her name? What if you were chased down by hordes of them?

    If every stranger I gave something to - a postage stamp, a quarter, a dollar, a pen, the time, a recipe, directions, advice - if they all came after me remembering every detail of the moment and asking for a personal connection - What would I do? I have always wondered about these people. Those moments were meaningful even if that's all they were. The heart does make gestures automatically, yet I might not want to know these people further. I might, I might not, if I was found by a stranger with an excellent memory, want to go back and observe that moment and whatever it might have created in the future.

AE

New message:

Lee Who Stung -
    Sorry for bothering you, just got word from None Of, that it was definitely not you giving me the jacket that day in Brooklyn. He can't remember who it was - and it doesn't really matter. I'm sorry for my weirdness (I guess). Perhaps I would not have read your book if my name wasn't in it. I have had a few interesting thoughts to meditate on because of this short mystery. –AE

New message

From: Lee Who Stung

  Well, apparently you were not the one to whom I gave my jacket, or else not I who gave you the jacket. I only met None Of recently, and though the name Your Business sounds familiar (did he go to Oxford?) I can't be sure. This entire correspondence has a Borgesian flavor, which of course I favor, but let's hope it doesn't get Kafkaesque. I said, 'exactly' for lack of a better word, not meaning to offend your modesty. Will you send a photo? Maybe you've done a self-portrait (you said in an earlier email that you were an artist?) You already know what I look like from head to toe (if you have one of my books), which seems miserably unfair to me, though of course that's not 'exactly' me, either....

LWS

New message

Lee Who Stung
  Jorge Luis Borges? I haven't read him. Yet. I like Kafka, why would that be worse? What is appealing about Borgesian particulars? Please explain. I didn't know our correspondence was going anywhere. "He never answered," I wrote of it. Maybe I'll have to revise. I was considering revising to make myself look better anyway, the whole correspondence makes me look like such a loser.
  Terribly unfair! If you can, describe yourself as you were at the time you gave your jacket away, and the whole event and context as it happened, and if you can also explain why you want my photo since we know it wasn't me, or it wasn't you, at the other end of the exchange. Anywise you will just have to wait till my book comes out with your name in it, and my photo on the back!

I'm going to NYC to see the Mythical Creatures exhibit. I'll be with my boyfriend and my daughter. If you want to set eyes on me, or bring a peace offering, who needs photographs?

How about Gogol's Overcoat? Maybe it's a mythical creature, like this jacket.

-Alice

p.s. what do you want me to call you? Are we friends, enemies, or metamorphosing into insects? Is it just the ghost of an overcoat chasing us? Anyway someone who looked a little like you, I don't remember much about his looks, gave me a jacket, a gift, just like that, out of the blue. So he must have liked me and it's wonderful to be liked, just like that, out of the blue. It was such a slim time there is not much to remember about it. The more I remember, perhaps the more I make up.

New message:

From: Lee Who Stung

I guess I'm someone who needs to judge a person with my eyes and not just by the exchange of words. I have long reached the place where I can choose who I associate with, and who I don't associate with, so I rarely correspond more than once with people outside my circle. Your name and energy were captivating, that was all. Anyway, if I am ever at a bookstore near wherever you live, maybe you'll surprise me and I'll unveil you saying, "And here's Alice Eckles, in the flesh." Perhaps you could wear the blue cardigan.

I'll be away from now on (on double sabbatical) Please be well, Alice Eckles.

Lee Who Stung

New message:

Attachment: photo of Alice, head shot

Lee Who Stung -
 Well, O.K., but I don't want to be introduced as a character, I want to be introduced as an author. I would consent to being introduced as both. I live in Vermont. I think I was warned of your email in my dream, in the dream the phone rang with a different tone for "high profile caller" I decided not to answer it. It would be better to listen to the message on the machine. Thanks for wishing me well, Lee Who Stung. Enjoy your traveling.

AE
 I noticed my neighbor's tomatoes weeks before all ripe and ready. They're never home, this is their summer place and tomatoes only ripen late in October when frost threatens in Vermont. "There's my grocery store," I thought, except I didn't need tomatoes that day. The days passed quickly and I forgot about the tomatoes.
 When my own tomatoes ripened I was going away on a trip and didn't need them that day. Tonight about dinnertime I thought, a grilled cheese sandwich with tomatoes and onion would be very good. I went out to fetch my tomatoes but the rabbit must have got there first, only green ones left. So it occurred to me to try my neighbor's garden, they weren't home. I have only talked to these neighbors once; the woman was hanging up newly bought flowers on the porch. "I buy all my plants in Canada," she told me "it's just a hop and a skip over the border and they are so much cheaper there." Just now I found a red tomato on the bare ground in her garden, the plant itself already dead, but the tomato was just right for my sandwich. Oh I am so wise I thought walking home with my prize. Wait; didn't I see another red tomato? I should have taken everything before the frost! Alas, I was thinking only of my sandwich, and this one was all I needed.

Ideas are the shirt of a man who is gone. What useless clothing these ideas that litter my desk.

Here is one of my ideas: What if a party had a group out of body experience. They would all be floating above the scene together watching their avatars below. Maybe that is what happens anyway. Maybe I am floating above every social situation and S. my sweetie is up here with me as we look down seeing ourselves and others act out the way that they are, from our opera seats. Our souls are not alone up here there are others, but privacy is natural to this world, and we are mostly aware of each other. At first I thought it was just me up here, but then I thought of S. and he was here. After that I knew others were also here. There is this duality in who we are, the people up here and the people down there, we are the same but different. I wonder how you see my avatar. It seems that the people down there are just symbols for us, and it wouldn't matter if you didn't think I was very attractive because our real selves are experienced up here in bodiless cuddling, our avatars are only chess pieces down there. We move our images below, accepting them as ours and loving them as one cares about characters in a movie, only more so. There is a sense of remove from reality, a feeling that if things go terribly wrong down there, we will still be up here enduring together. The world is a stage but up here is forever, even if we are down there acting on the stage, we are above it all, we may act in other plays when this one is over.

Here is another one of my ideas: Today things were just falling apart. My hands were klutzy, putting things in the wrong place. Everything I touched seemed to fall off. I was very busy and hardly noticed. I worked twice as hard because the world was functioning half as well. Then it struck me, the world was falling apart and if I didn't stop the trend there would be nothing but rubble in days. Just as I realized this, a coffee cup fell out of the cupboard. It was my favorite coffee cup, a large pale yellow diner mug. There was a chip missing on the rim where it hit the toaster oven. It was just a small chip, I could have overlooked it.

Then I realized that I had to stop the direction things were going in or there would be nothing left. So I got on my hands and knees and searched till I found the small yellow chip of porcelain and I got some super glue and glued the piece back in. I saved the world with that small mending; I changed the direction things were going in. It was just that one coffee cup broken or whole that stood between a falling apart world and a held together one.

Another idea:
      What if in the course of aging, lets say we were all quite old, I knew that I would have a few surprising years of youth before abruptly returning to the age of my contemporaries, do you think I would keep my place among my friends and wait it out - or abandon them and seize the power of my youth? Nothing can hold back youth, even a flukish burst of it that comes at the wrong time, that's the nature of youth. I would give up decades of investment in my life, unable to pretend I don't have this new fresh zest, I'd start over. Do you think my old friends would forgive me? Do you think they would take me back once I regained my tired gray look, and slower pace? After I had once abandoned them in disgust? I don't know, they might, but how then would I feel? I might rather be in a tragedy where I cannot return, except to the echo of my own betraying. In such a tragedy one keeps youth close to the heart. A horse would express this perfectly. My horse, wanders into the highway wearing blinders, cars swerve around him, he is lucky, oblivious, a wonder, generating concern. In the dream he wasn't my horse, but in a dream isn't everything yours?

Another idea:
      I was going to offer a class without time lumps, as a convenience to college students. Everything takes so much longer to learn and gets confusing when historical information clumps up like to like, but always in new whimsical ways, right when you are trying to get from here

to there and then you can't because you have to sort out the bunched up strands of different times. Of course they are all one time, we think, but even if that is so, the thing is so infinite it cannot be taught as one thing. Somehow if we could teach a class without time lumps, what a convenience that would be!

12

The seeker who meets a face of negativity and confusion has good luck; this scary monster is a guardian who wants to chase away the obstacles to your finding spiritual truth. As I observe my actions, thoughts, and words, I see how I resist my highest good and create a monster. At the very same time I am healing and changing. There is nothing wrong with the way things are. I can accept myself burdens and all, if those burdens are there I can bear them. Not to worry. Slowly and gently, I work myself out of all bondage. There is a two-ness, the resister and the healer are the same person walking together, in friendship.

November

Nothing really happens in November except lots of weekends away traveling, the agony and finally acceptance of "A Week In The Life Of Alice" by Seattle Review, the bread baking revolution, a fellow driver gives me the finger, one afternoon spent in the cafes of Bristol Vermont, buying lingerie with S., receiving the terrible news that my car needs $1,500 in repairs, painful eye heals by morning, and you'll find a few other things.

We are considering joining Metta Earth; we could buy land and build our cordwood house here. The room smells like wool. The fleece shorn from sheep is hanging up to dry. G. walked us through the house – which is to be the communal space – but is now also their home. Later they plan to build a house nearby, and this space would have a yoga room, office, library, guest room or rooms, kitchen, dining room and two bathrooms. After the house tour we sorted through a large quantity of rose hips that G. and friends had harvested from the coast of Maine. We sat at the kitchen table with bags, a bowl and a bucket. The ones that were good for freezing went into bags, the ones that were good for eating right away went into a big dish in the middle, and the ones that were good enough for chickens into the bucket on the floor. We talked mostly about the rose hips themselves. Then we had rose hip tea and we talked more about Metta Earth, and ideas about the kind of community it would be and what people hoped for and were interested in, also any concerns about living in such a community. I liked the feeling that this community could be whatever those who were attracted to it interpreted it to be.

S. stayed Sunday to help raise the barn. I would have loved to have stayed and watched how the timber pieces were notched, pegged, and fitted together, but I figured if I layered my sweater and vest over S., at least one of us could stay and help, without freezing.

Last weekend we were at Metta Earth, the weekend before that we visited my daughter at her college in New York City. We went to the Mythical Creatures exhibit at the Natural History Museum. The weekend before that we went to a Beekeepers Association meeting in Massachusetts, where S. was giving a talk on natural beekeeping, the subject of his book by the same title. I helped him sell the books, I helped drive, and I helped share the fun. I enjoyed seeing his books sell like hot cakes.

Now, this weekend we are in Maine. We drove here towing a trailer behind S.'s veggie oil car to pick up beekeeping equipment at Humble Abode, thereby saving hundreds of dollars on shipping. We stayed with the sister of S's friend and her husband. I liked them. I hope the feeling was mutual. I feel dismayed and confused about all things social, especially lately. A friend once said: "You are bold when you should be timid and timid when you should be bold." Camden, Maine is very pleasant. I hope I will like Metta Earth as much. I am responsible for the architecture of my life.

This coming weekend we are driving to Ohio for another Beekeeping Association meeting where S. will talk about natural beekeeping and sell his book by the same title. I will help.

Let me tell you what I wish for right now: I wish that I would get warm emails from certain editors I have written to recently. In these emails I would be forgiven for all my wrong doings, submitting simultaneously, forgetting to include a S.A.S.E., not recording who I sent what to, and writing weird emails to the wrong people instead of proceeding in a normal business like way. I would like to be forgiven and excused by anyone who has heard my pitiful whining about being an unpublished writer. I would like it if I were shown special respect in some concrete way.

We are staying with the treasurer of the Ohio Beekeeping Association, and his wife. "How long have you two been married?" she asked me as we were chatting in the kitchen. "We're not actually married." I replied. "Not officially!" S. chimed in from the living room.

A piece of my writing was accepted and no big deal was made of my weird emails and my not following instructions. It was a flattering email, so unexpected and such a relief. I think I am onto something with these nonfiction essays. The reader likes to have something to hang onto. I can be that, I can act it out, but I can't paint the illusion of it. I'm a sculptural writer, I write the props and act the life.

When you are driving, what matters emotionally when someone honks at you or gives you the finger is

"Who is right?" Yesterday after dropping off some clothing in one of those yellow save-the-planet-drop-off boxes I pulled into traffic, but apparently I did not slam my hatch closed hard enough because the spare tire on the iron gate came unlatched swinging open on it's hinge. I stopped and the van behind me stopped and waited, so I figured they were going to let me get out and do what I had to do. So I got out of the car and slammed my hatch shut. As the older woman in a van passed me she honked and gave me the finger. At first this bothered me, because I am not a great driver, and I am tired of getting harassed about it, but then I decided that she was just an old crank and I was just doing what had to be done. One can't drive around with the gate open, and the spare swinging all around. She had already stopped and waited for me to fix the problem, it isn't my fault she was irritated by one of life's little snags.

    Earlier I had just been in the co-op getting a sandwich for the road. The young man making my sandwich handed it to me with such a smile. I wondered if it came from his youth, this uplifted spirit. There was an older couple ordering their sandwich at the same time I was ordering mine. They wore very sour faces and were arguing about what would never do, never work, how the whole sandwich thing was futile. It seemed ridiculously dire. I didn't know how they would resolve their food problem. So I just ignored them, as if they were crazy, and so did the young man who happily kept making sandwiches.

    I had a meager dinner, there's not much food in the house. Apart from yogurt with fruits and nuts that I'll have for breakfast tomorrow, there are essentially no more meals in the house. Thursday is my bread-baking day, but so far I have only baked bread on one Thursday. Tomorrow, Thursday, there is supposed to be a snowstorm. I thought about cutting my hair today. There are many reasons I should cut my hair. Long hairs are always falling out; everywhere I go I leave long hairs behind. I have hair in my bed, hair on my clothes, hair in my car, hair on the floor, hair stuck to my socks. This is reason enough, but also it is dangerous in lovemaking where I can get accidentally pinned down by my hair and somehow not want to say anything about it. Moreover there is the matter of split ends; I am very distracted by them. Whenever I am alone I find myself sifting through my hair, picking off split ends. So I should cut my hair to a less distracting length. Every time I try, I think, "No, it is too beautiful just the way it is, even with split ends, even with a little grey coming in" My hair is a dark sleek background for my face that seems cozy and flattering with the different ways that it falls. Instead of cutting it I spend an hour or two singling out split ends and cutting them off. I have this memory from the time shortly after my second daughter was born, and I had joined a mother's play group. I felt very out of place. The only thing I had in common with these women was that I also had a baby. I was poor; they were rich. I was young; they were middle aged. I had short hair; they had long hair. The things these women talked about seemed far from my world. For example, one woman with very long hair had a problem with split ends, but she didn't want to cut her hair. Another woman suggested she go to her hairdresser because she knew how to remove split ends one by one so that you didn't have to cut your hair any shorter. She warned us, "It costs a fortune." The woman was very grateful for this advice and said it was definitely worth it.

  This coming Sunday is the anniversary of the day S. and I first met. It will be a year on Sunday that we have been together. After Sunday everyday of the year will be revisited by our togetherness. Last Thanksgiving just after our first date, I dated an old friend of his, I didn't know then that he was an old friend of his, I was just following through on a mate selection method I had decided on. The method was that I had to meet three new people at a coffee shop in quick succession, then choose one to meet again, perhaps for dinner, then see what happens next. S. fit into my method, because I was just about to go for a second date with one of the three new people, but the guy cancelled on me. So, S. who I had to say, "No" to before, because of my method, which stipulates only three candidates at a time, was available to take the other guy's place. S. did not have a picture to go with his ad on the local paper's internet dating site, but I had started to care less about that. Guys definitely choose women by how they look, but they are very shy about letting women do the same. I liked what S. had to say in his ad. and I thought I might like him. There were three things that made me wonder if S. might be a woman though. First he seemed too thoughtful, and not idiotic enough to be a man. Secondly he listed his height as five feet four inches, and thirdly I had been getting attention from women. At first I was ambivalent in my ever-changing ad. about if I was seeking a friend or a mate – did I have to decide? Yes, I decided I had to decide, so I decided, mate. I was excited and happy to see he was a man. I had to stick with my method, three candidates at a time, so I made a date with a new person for Thanksgiving coffee. S. was still my favorite after that. On our second date he gave me a rose, which as my oldest grown daughter pointed out when she saw it, is a little forward for a second date. I brought a gift too, which was an inspired last minute decision that probably made me late, and maybe he had to go buy the rose to pass the time so as not to be depressed that I was late. Though, now that I know him better, I think he probably wasn't sweating it.

  A flower represents transience. It blooms and dies. I was wondering if I should just go with the transience; spread the petals in my bed before they dried, or…or what? I expressed my concern over the symbolic wilting of the rose. He suggested drying it. "I don't know about dried flowers," I said. "What don't you know about them?" S. said. One of his Christmas gifts to me last year was dried flowers in a little basket that I hang by my back door. He is very thoughtful about gifts.

The day before yesterday was Thursday, my bread-baking day, and I did make bread. It was the second Thursday in my bread baking revolution. For our one-year anniversary, one year from the day we met, S. gave me some sour dough bread starter. I thought this was very fabulous; starter to celebrate our start. The word fabulous reminds me of the blueberry mead we had last night. I am really quite extremely fond of him and the blueberry mead was really good too.

I am sitting at a little table in back, hidden behind a shelf of cereals. I have never been to this store before. I had to do a little research about me "where I am" for my daily journal. I was going to go outside and look up at the front of the building to find the name of the store for today's entry. On my way I met my lifetime companion who is giving samples of his honey at the store today. He asked me if I would like a sample. I said yes, my last sample had just run out and I told him I was doing a little research for my writing which is all about where I am and what I'm doing and so I asked, "What's the name of this store?" "Mountain Greens in Bristol Vermont" he said and I scurried back to my laptop behind the cereal boxes. The backs of the cereal boxes face me, I see words like: Natures Path, Eating Lean, Cinnamon Puffins. This is a very pleasant store in my view, not too crowded, good organic local wholesome foods, good music, bulk items, easygoing people.

There was a girl, one of the first shoppers of the morning, who was very noticeable to look at she had blond and black hair, sort of striped, and on this cold day she was wearing shorts, and had beautiful tattoos on her tan legs. I wondered if the shorts were tattoos too and maybe even the tan. I wasn't sure where reality ended and illusion began with this girl but she seemed like a serious type, with a real life and real concerns and happy moments. On the way out I almost bumped into her again. She commented that, "We keep doing that" This gave me the chance to comment on her shorts, " I can't believe you are wearing shorts, it's so cold, but I guess you have your core warm" she had on a down vest and sweater. Then she told me she had to wear shorts because she had just gotten the tattoos and you have to keep them uncovered for a few days. I complimented her on her tattoos, which really were quite attractive; they were large and bold, like an Eskimo design. The shapes were like the holes in a violin. Anyway it was cool to learn something new about tattoos. I would never want a tattoo myself, because I don't have the skin for it, and I don't like to spend money for pain. Sometimes I admire the art though on other people.

    I have here at my desk-of-the-moment, a leaf. I met the girl on the way to the car to get the leaf, which is today my thinking object, the way Chinese scholars used to have a philosophers stone to inspire or focus their thoughts. The leaf caught my eye yesterday when I was checking on the bees with my lifetime companion, putting insulation under the lids of the hives. This oak leaf caught my eye because it is shaped a little differently than most oak leaves and I thought the variation was quite beautiful. The top part of the leaf is exaggerated so that three parts spread expressively like wings and tail feathers; the lower part of the leaf is less developed, thinner like a neck for the raised gesture. There is something else strange about this leaf. On the lower part, the less developed part, and if you don't know what an oak leaf looks like you should go find out right now, or you have nothing to base my description on, on the lower part there are four holes, open sections between veins, and these holes are perfectly symmetrical to each other. Like when you roll dice and get a four, that is the four at the bottom of this leaf. To me it doesn't look accidental. I immediately thought of tribal scarification, I had discovered a leaf that had purposely sought meaningful beautification, to set itself apart among leaves to show it's status, or place among trees, or tribal affiliation with this sign on its body.

Outside the store also on my way to the car to get my thinking leaf from the car, I saw some maple saplings coming through the hedge. On the leaves of this maple I saw black spots of fungus that I have heard about. I heard this fungus is killing trees in Maine and that Maples are migrating north due to the warming climate. We talked of the possibility of losing maples, and maple syrup in Vermont. The black fungus was not visually pleasing; the saplings seemed sad and unhealthy, it was kind of sad to see, like a bag lady outside the store, an unfortunate.
    I was wondering though, while I was cleaning houses, remember that's one of my jobs, whether it made any difference that I saw and appreciated the art in the house. As I passed a carved wooden turtle made of a tree burl, I couldn't help petting the turtle as if it were real, a pet turtle. A burl is a place on a tree where a fungus has made the tree grow a lump. Some people hollow out the burls to make beautiful wooden bowls of them. Anyway, as I touched the turtle I could feel that he was not dusty, much of cleaning is done by feel. My feet and hands feel irregularities of texture and know this is the grit of daily life that is to be swept up, scrubbed off, or dusted away. I wondered if this seeing, not of the daily grit, but of the collections people keep, their beautiful things and keepsakes is part of my service. Do I also to groom these things with my eyes, as if all these things were alive and by my seeing them the dust is peeled off?
    " I know her," the boy said to his mother. They were all sitting in the atrium at the children's table in tiny chairs eating lunch. I was leaving because I had overheard the mother say, "Oh there's only one table" I was sitting at that table writing very fast everything that I was thinking. I saw the boy out of the corner of my eye. I knew when he said he knew me that he meant he knew me as the woman who was sitting at the table writing. He knew me from there, yes, when I came back in again, it was the third time he had seen me, he definitely knew me this time. Even though I had never looked at them I was trying to give the family

their privacy- and the grown up table. They seemed happy at the children's table.

I went for a walk it was a cold but clear and beautiful day, a very pleasant town I was deciding. I went on to a bakery, with just enough money to buy an oatmeal raisin cookie; they had good water for free. There was a man playing the ukulele, he had his case open and it had a fair amount of cash in it. He started packing up soon after I sat down. I sort of wanted to ask him some questions about the ukulele. I think he was ready to get out of there and have lunch and I was only wanting to ask certain questions without having to get into a long chat because I have writing to do. I was thinking how promising this seems the fine sunny spot; I was thinking maybe I should play the ukulele; its smaller than a guitar and maybe just as good. I don't play the guitar but maybe instead I should try the ukulele, if it's just as good... There are some prints hanging on the wall, they are pretty good, and as you know I am a printmaking teacher, if not an actual printmaker, ha ha, so this is another sign of quality to me, I am thinking that this is a very nice and pleasant town that I might want to live near. Metta Earth where my lifetime companion and I are considering building our house is just up the hill, or mountain. I've heard though that there is a surveillance camera on top of the church and that images of goings on in town go straight to the police station. That is pretty weird. They say there was some trouble with teenage vandals. Everything looks picturesque from my bakery window.

My treasures are my observations. Once I saw a blue dress, on a manikin outside a vintage store. I looked at the dress, and went into the store. The woman inside said, "That dress would fit you, you should try it on." She said that many women were watching this dress. She said her experience in retail had shown her that energy gathers around an admired object. One person admires something then more people do, and this energy of desire starts to build up around an object, it becomes "hot" like this dress. It pulls in new admirers. She made me feel I would be the lucky winner if I bought it. Not all women who admire the dress could buy it. Since it is a vintage dress it requires a slim old-fashioned figure. Eventually a moth ate it, but mostly other women admired me in the dress a few times before that. It was a dress that required old fashioned posture, I could not take great strides and I had to cross my legs when sitting down.

I shared my leaf with my art classes, since I encourage them to share their art related experiences from the week at the beginning of each class. Some children reported building snow men, or finding ice crystals on the play ground, one child mentioned seeing Barcelona on T.V. where Picasso lived and Gaudi's architecture resides. Some children had strange things to report about trees they had been watching, and delightful discoveries made with mud, the group's collective knowledge of mud was quite high, some children wanted to talk about posters on the wall, a Louise Nevelson sculpture and an alligator mask from Africa.

It's scary to buy lingerie. I don't know why it should be scary but it is. When I came out of the dressing room the sales woman was wrapping it up and I said, "I'm the same size as his wife, so it works out for me to try on stuff for his wife"- "Just kidding" I quickly added That's when my knee caps started to tremble. In truth we are just a normal couple, he's my boyfriend and he suggested getting me lingerie for Christmas, so we stopped into this local establishment called, Queen Annie's Lace. I asked S., "What is lingerie, and when do you wear it? To bed? So I'll take off all my clothes and then put on these little things to get in bed and take them off again?" My boyfriend just asked the sales woman almost exactly the same question. The sales woman said lingerie could be worn like underwear or even; a camisole like this (she gestured) can be worn as a shirt. I said I liked the idea of things that could be worn as clothes or at least underclothes. I picked out a brown camisole with a shelf bra and some undies. I could see that my boyfriend was not too excited about my selection though, he seemed unsure of the color brown. "Brown looks good on me, brown is one of my colors," I said. I also like black and he much preferred black, so I got black. I really think I look a lot better in brown. I know that black is considered sexy and if it's not sexy to your boyfriend, why wear it? It was his suggestion to buy lingerie; therefore it was his desire to see me in it, therefore why wear brown if he thinks I look prettier in black? It seems to me that this is a big scary deal. Why does black turn men on? Is there a biological reason? I worry that this need for lingerie that he has expressed by offering to buy me lingerie may mean he is not satisfied with my look. I should ask him why he wanted to buy me lingerie. When it comes to personal appearance, little things can seem like a big personal deal. I think we had better get the black camisole AND brown one. Can you teach someone to love the color brown? Can you teach them that brown is sexy? Brown is warm and soft like an animal, like my hair, like the woods. My blue eyes, my pale skin, my brown hair, this is my color trio. He did not go for the idea of buying a black one and a brown one, and he did not believe me when I told him that brown is the new pink. I pleaded with him to adore me in brown, but he said I could buy brown things for myself. Which is true, and I do, my bathing suit is brown. Black or brown it is a very small matter especially when I like black as well as brown. Black matches my lashes and eyebrows. It turns out my car needs some very expensive repairs. So that kind of highlights how trivial the matter of black or brown lingerie is, at least that became the score in my mind. No, I started thinking about much bigger matters after the car news came in, and forgave him for not seeing how attractive I am in brown lingerie. That was small brown potatoes. I started worrying about how unsustainable my current life is, and if I were able to make a more sustainable life with him I worried about losing everything I have worked so hard to achieve if it didn't work out. Finally I have one last question to ask, does he really love me, the way he would want to love someone who he would spend the rest of his life with? Can his answer be yes, even if we disagree on which color of lingerie looks best on me? Maybe even if he doesn't totally appreciate my style, maybe that ultimate kind of love could still be there.

    My eyes are very sensitive. It hurts most when I shut my eyes and try to go to sleep. I whimpered, I remember, in bed before I fell asleep, I felt like a dog, my submissive belly exposed, but not accepted. I caught myself in a painful dying howl. It is Thanksgiving night. If I were a dog my situation would be intolerable, but I am a human, and humans sometimes like to spend Thanksgiving alone. I stayed up late looking in the papers and online for a new car. Last night when I picked up my car from Midas, after they told what was wrong with my car and how much it was going to cost, I realized this car is the hole in my bucket. The car, that is what's ruining me, and I can't afford to buy a new one. It's miserable news to try to digest alone on Thanksgiving, but this morning my eye is healed, miraculously.

    "Before I met you," he said, "I made a list of everything I wanted in a woman."

    "So did I." I said.

    "In a woman?" he asked

    "No, in a man" I said

    "I'll show you mine if you show me yours" he said

    I think I threw my list away because it was embarrassing. Does S. match the list? S. is not an artist, that's the only thing from my wish list I can remember that doesn't match S. I also specified no facial hair. Many men in Vermont have facial hair. Facial hair is only natural for men, so I felt bad about that being on my list, and that's one of the reasons I tossed the list. S. does not have facial

hair anyway.
    Here is my list from memory:
- Nonsmoker
- No facial hair
- Healthy
- No more than 5 years older than me
- An artist of some kind
- Generous
- Gentle
- Ready for a relationship
- Able to communicate and work out problems
- Intelligent
- College graduate
- Financially healthy
- Someone I can do things with that interest me
- Someone my daughters like
- Cute
- Compassionate to all beings
- Enjoys nature

    I remembered today that, "nurturing" was on the list. I wanted a nurturing man! Well, that I got in S.

    "Creative genius" or any other kind of genius was not on the list of things I was looking for in a man. I wanted him to be smart, to share my love of learning, but not a genius, somehow I decided they were a bad lot as husbands, more trouble than they were worth (a terrible thing to say). Someone more well balanced I told myself. I am happy with my choice.

    I have a safety net now, my house in North Hero. If something goes wrong, it will be my safety net. If nothing goes wrong it is still my safety net. We are buying a truck together now. Buying the truck together is the first step out on the tight rope.

    The truck is to replace my Kia Sportage. The Kia, even a 2000 with low miles, is more than twice the cost to maintain than my last car. My last car, a 95 Suzuki Sidekick, was great till it rusted out. S. said he was thinking about getting a truck to build our house with, and I suggested that we didn't need three cars between us, we should try to get down to just one. So he is going to buy the truck and convert it to run on veggie oil, and we will share his car and the truck. I'll sell my car. This should lower my gas and car maintenance expenses. When the house is built we could get down to one car.

"We've known each other all this time, and this has never happened before", he says moving closer.

"It takes me a while to warm up." I say commenting on before.

Then suddenly I am very hot. I pull my tangerine angora sweater over my head, and get sort of stuck there inside it. I think of asking for his help pulling it off, but realize that would be a bad idea. I get the sweater off and I lay back on the couch. I feel a longing and attraction, but I won't speak to it. I fall into a trancelike state, while he waits expectantly for my response. There is a strong trance inducing vibration coming from my abdomen and from my heart. My hands are on my heart. My heart impresses a grimace on my face.

I want to see depth in the forest as light nimbly weaves though the homogenous distance of limbs. I want to see faces again like I did before I learned the multiplication tables. I've been searching for my true vision since the gods stole my glasses last August, they did, right off my head. I was looking cool, with the prescription sunglasses propped on top of my head. They wanted to play with them too, but they never gave them back, and they never give things back - perhaps only when you die.

I can't see "You" and I'm not happy about it. I used to be happy about it, I wanted to be shielded from your jaws, but now I find it irritating that across a crowded room you are a blur. It's boring - I don't care if you scowl or smile at me I just want to see you.

What if I wrote a bestseller about a metaphorical

change in vision and published the book under a fake name? Then incognito I would devote my life to going to book groups discussing the book, not as the author, but as fellow reader, pulling out the fine threads, and trying to bring up the healing vibration of the book with a massive weaving of group generated enlightenment. Then perhaps, the author could see faces in real life, just like before the multiplication tables.

13

In the worst of times, like thief sentenced to be boiled in oil, do not lose possession of yourself. Write a poem! Not too long, something to make you feel good, a clever compliment to you and all your kind. The purpose of life is to love yourself, no matter what happens, and in your own way to make the best of any situation. This is the real gospel written by a thief: Always look on the bright side of life!

Once when I was a child I watched the kitchen fill with water. I was home alone witnessing a disaster; the dishwasher was seriously malfunctioning. I didn't know what to do and it occurred to me that it isn't everyday that you get to watch such a fountain exploding in the kitchen. So I sat up on the kitchen counter top and watched a while. I thought about the end of the world and the different ways it was supposed to come. You can't do anything about the end of the world, so I suppose there nothing wrong with enjoying the show, there may be many beautiful things to see in a time of destruction.

Holiday Message

I was climbing the ladder to hang a giant snowflake one of my 3rd graders had just made, when I had a vision. The vision was a sticker on top of the ladder. In the sticker there was a bright yellow woman in high heels and a narrow skirt climbing the ladder, she was circled and crossed in red, to show that you shouldn't climb ladders in high heels. I was dressed appropriately in jeans, but female teachers often dress as if they worked in an office. I immediately thought of other warning signs, like one to prevent scarf wearers from letting their scarves get caught in machinery. One child asked me last time I climbed the ladder, hanging their wrapping paper up to dry, if I was afraid to climb the ladder. I said no, I'm not afraid because I don't go above the second to the top rung, just like it says on the ladder, and I know it's a safe ladder when used as directed. "Also" I added, " I'm not afraid of heights." Many children also volunteered that they were not afraid of heights either.

    I was driving to the college to meet some students for evaluations, when a thankful thought came to me. I was thankful that my life mate has decided to save me from the end of the world, flattered too. I was thinking how an acquaintance I once knew, who counseled people in crisis on how to get their shit together, said that most people just ignore their problems. "People say," he continued, " that you shouldn't just ignore your problems, but I see people's problems do go away when they simply ignore them." I personally feel I've gotten half way to concurring my problems by ignoring them, which means worrying less and feeling better about myself. The time has come when there are no chips left in the bag and that simply can't be ignored. So I am feeling glad that my life mate in his wisdom is preparing for peak oil, global warming, economic collapse, and is going to save me from the coming doom. I have never been one to believe in doom. Well, I do believe in it but I try not to think about it, I don't want to be sad, or overwhelmed. I am savoring the last drops of the good life and postponing worry. Nonetheless, I had this thought as I was driving, "The time is now" Not just for me to convert my car to veggie oil, but for my sister too. Not just for me to grow and save my own food, but for my sister too. I see in her a mirror of necessity, how our cars bleed us, and we don't have long before we faint, if this keeps up. I am an indulgent person. I ask my life mate, "Why can't you just spend two weekends here in the summer and we can go kayaking, and drink pina coladas on the beach?" I thought I'd buy him a kayak. He said, "No, I have to build a house this summer I won't have time." I talked him into one weekend. Maybe he is right, you see, I had this feeling while I was driving of feeling grateful that he believes in the coming doom and is going to save me, kind of flattered too. While I was out, since I am an indulgent person, I bought two high quality delicious chocolate bars, and a bag of high quality vegetable chips. By high quality, I mean organic and expensive. If my life mate were there with me he might have suggested that maybe I should save my money, he might have suggested, "Chocolate bars or bag of chips, why both?" He would have said you can eat when we get home. He'd offer to cook. He'd offer to drive. I would have conceded the chips easily since I bought the chocolate first. Just his offer to cook or to drive would have bolstered me enough not to miss the chips. That would have saved me three dollars. They tried to charge me five dollars for the chips, but the manager was behind me in line, she let me use her card to get the sale price.

I was in the store, the bank of Shaws, filling out a deposit form, when I over heard a conversation between a male and female stocker in the cosmetics department. They were talking about their children and the state of education both public and private. It seemed like a rather high level discussion for a couple of stockers. Then I thought of ways to intensify the strangeness as if I were going to make a movie of it. I would find conversations in high-level sectors and have them spoken by people in working class positions. I would make it look like the little people were running the world and they didn't care at all that they were little people. It is an alarming cultural indicator that a bystander like me would find it strange that ordinary people make high-level executive decisions. It means that normal doesn't seem normal anymore, like we have the wrong normal.

In the other store where I bought the take-the-edge-off-the-end-of-the-world-chocolate, I asked a man who was filling his bag with oats, if he knew where the yeast was. He did not but suggested that they might be in that little cooler with refrigerated nuts and stuff. I looked and there they were. "I found them with your tip" I told him as he was still suggesting places where the yeast might be. Back in the parking lot it was very icy and snowy and I was trying to rock my car out of its parking place. I noticed a man sleeping in the darkness of a car parked next to mine. The man got out and made a signal that he would push my car. I fumbled for a signal and came back with thumbs up. Whenever people do small things for me or I do small things for them, even though it is just by chance, or maybe especially because it is by chance it seems special. I believe in the power of subtleties. Very small things matter, like a toehold if you are climbing. I don't believe in magic, not the magic eight ball, dowsing, or positive thinking. I believe in subtle powers, like that, "In your heart you know", and that with attention you can know, that you know, more than you know. I believe that by taking hold of the power of the small you can change things. No matter how little you can do to show them, intentions really do matter. I don't believe that this is magic, because it makes sense that things would work this way, but I do think it is beautiful and therefore magical.

  Earth, I wonder what it means to people on other planets who are born under this star. What story would explain earth in their sky? What personality traits would children born under the influence of earths twinkle have? See I am part of this dust, the dust that shines in the night, and I want to know light years away which children have my traits, and how, how does my star influence people on other planets who are born under it. I am part of this star, the earth. One cannot be born under their own star; one cannot know the influence of self, until people on other planets explain their universe with you in it.

14

There is a woman you will find platonic friendship with. She has written a book of life, it is not written in English though. It is written in life, it contains nothing mundane. To understand the meaning of life you could try to play her hundred poets game. She will not share a shred of explanation though. She holds tightly a blank piece of paper on which anything could be written a healing herbal formula, or perhaps love poems. Poetic intuition is all that is needed to receive your transmission of a special idea-o-gram.

To have wisdom, knowledge, and joy in one garden is her example of self-reliance. You may not like her; she is impatient and hides her emotions from others. Undermining this aloofness is an urge that she has to communicate with you.

Ice Fishing

I pretend to know nothing about ice fishing; no more than the other civilized people who consider it to be an odd pastime for - dare I say hicks? I do know a little something about ice fishing. You don't get to know about other people unless you don't have to be the type of person you are, so because I am a curious shape shifting person, and also because two lonely people happened to meet, I went ice fishing once with a local guy. What I know from this, that I don't admit when the subject comes up, is that ice fishing is fun. It's hard for city people to understand ice fishing, they think it's a drinking shack on ice. What I don't want to tell them, because I would have to admit how I found out, is that if they actually went ice fishing they would find it to be fun.

First, the fish, the fish just jump on the hook one after the other, there's no waiting around, not like summer fishing. It's exciting, you grab those wiggly fish and well I can't remember if I took the hook out myself or not, but I grabbed many fish, and my mittens got wet, and that is the only bad thing about ice fishing, cold hands. Another exciting thing about ice fishing is walking on the ice, it's a different landscape, you have been forbidden to walk on it all summer, but here it is, you could walk over to that island, this bright sunny day. You can get sunburned out there, a real vitamin D opportunity, dead in winter. Also it can be windy and it is fun to see other people's fishing huts get blown away when you are happy to sit on a bucket in the open air by a hole. There is a special drill for making the ice hole, it is about 5 inches wide, the ice is really thick. When you see how thick the ice is you're not afraid of falling through. The other thing about ice fishing is the fish. You take them home, spread newspapers out on the kitchen table. This is how you fillet a fish: You hold it down with your hand over the head and cut from under the head to the tail as close to the line of fish bones as you can. Then you turn it over and do the same thing to the other side. Then you hold the fish skin at the top and run the knife under. You do this to both fillets to get the skin off. Toss the fillets on a plate for frying and roll up the discards in the newspaper for trash. Then start again on the next fish, and the next, and the next. That's the way I saw it done. Then you bread the fish and deep-fry it, and everybody just eats tons of fresh fish. You should have a lot of people over to share the bounty. It's great. I know maybe your not supposed to eat so much fish anymore because of pollution, but it sure feels good to do it and those fish sure look good to eat from the moment they come out of the ice hole to the moment they become dinner. I went out the next day after this first ice fishing experience and bought myself some ice-fishing mittens. The sales person at North Face didn't know what to recommend for ice fishing, he said that no one really ice fishes they just sit around drinking and it doesn't matter what mittens you get. I saw no drinking till the fish were served, and then it was all Pabst Blue Ribbon which although I've never tasted it, I'm sure is a bad yucky beer. I like Guinness or Otter Creek something like that, or red wine. I bought black down filled mittens with rubberized palms for gripping wet fish. I never went ice fishing again.

  I suppose I could, I have the right kind of bucket to sit on, a good pair of mittens, and in the shed I have some fishing poles I have never used. These along with the bucket, and many other useful things came with the house when I bought it from a Canadian. There was a deep fryer too, but I threw that out, little did I know. The only thing I don't have is the ice drill, and I could borrow one if I went on the right day. There is an elderly man who lives near here. I talked to him once and learned that years ago he got laid off, and since there is no work to be had on the island, he began ice fishing on a more full time basis and now he sells his fish to a store in New York. Fish from the Vermont side of the lake must be considered better. He has a little four-wheeler he drives to the point and he sets up his bucket out there. I could go out, when I see him out, take my bucket and pole, and borrow his ice drill, then set up nearby to fish. For the amount of fish I eat I wouldn't have to sit out there two seconds, or I could stay out a little longer, fill the freezer and be set for winter. Most ice fishers would think that was dumb, because you'd miss out on all those wonderful ice fishing days and, "Would you eat frozen fish, when you could have fresh?"

  Way back in my family there were fishermen and fisher women. My mother will still fish if she gets the chance. In the summer, in my grandparent's trailer on the lake in Farmerville, Louisiana, we used to have great fish fries. I myself sometimes set a fish trap and checked it now and then. My grandfather was the only one who cleaned fish, so after he died fishing became sort of like the appendix in our family. Crab, shrimp, and crawdads were also sought by various members of the family. Myself, I caught bees among the four leaf clovers that I gathered to provide luck for my future. The Bees were set free after a period of confinement in a jar. I had a friend who liked to catch bees, and since I hunted for four leaf clovers I figured there was enough overlap in our interests for us to play together. I was only six. My big sister didn't allow me to come with her hunting crawdads.

We moved from Louisiana to Kansas, my grandfather died and the culture of fishing, the idea that it was a normal thing to do, became pretty much extinct for me.

I was secretly convinced in early adolescence, after we moved to Kansas, that because I had the secret knowledge of fishing way back in my background, I was smarter than everyone else. Outwardly the opposite seemed true, and it was a little frustrating for me that my superior intelligence was a big secret.

I am a gentle and cultured person, a thinking woman, and none of this goes against ice fishing, I just wanted to be honest about this issue of class, to protest against the snobbery, as I have neglected to do before, whenever the topic came up.

Time is a very important number. The problem is it really isn't a number at all. We don't live in abstractions, though the world may be abstract. We will have to learn to cut this number, time, both ways. Time must be defined if only to keep yours safe in the bank, where only you can allocate it. Words, numbers, and all forms of language have the power of suggestion, and move the tiny wheels of our lives into action. I crossed out with a black sharpie the words on my shampoo bottle that said, "For dull and lifeless hair". I listened to a CD of Tibetan singing bowls that advertised itself as healing all the charkas. I doubted that it would be healing, but I listened to the CD before bed – and in the morning I found my glasses! They had been lost for two days and I was mad for them.

The Deadline Is July 21st

I have three months to write about death. I have delayed long enough. It means, I'm alive, I'm alive as a writer; my dream is alive.

Death attacks physically. We see death coming as we age, or sometimes with early battle scars, or when death strikes close. Gnashing and digesting body by body, Death knows everyone eventually, and gives our bodies back to the earth. The whole material world falls into the mouth of death, the ultimate eater. Mushrooms in the ground that no scientist can classify are like flora in Death's intestine, knowing something intermediary about life and death. My little spark of life is part of a cosmic creator fire and has made active at least some of its purpose here on earth.

Life is a game and it has rules. One of the rules is that you have to avoid death as long as possible. It is true that death is sort of an illusion, just like the rules of the game are just made up, but these illusions serve to motivate us and make the game fun. So if you start to say that this blood is just ketchup, then pain, the enforcer of this rule that you must try to stay alive, comes and grips you, saying, "Death is real, get your butt back in there or I'll squeeze the living daylights out of you"

Death took my little turtle first, a turtle that a very special friend gave me before she moved away. I was only five years old. On the first day of kindergarten I had to leave the turtle alone unattended. I thought the turtle would enjoy the sun, so I put his little red bowl filled with water and one sunning rock on the windowsill and walked to school. I thought of my turtle often during the day. When I came home I cried because the turtle was dead. There was no water in the bowl; he was all dried up. I asked my father what happened to the water and he explained that the water evaporated. "Evaporated" is a big word for a five year old but that was no excuse for me because, I instantly remembered, only a few days before my dad showed me how to walk to school, and on that walk I inquired about a certain puddle that had been there the day before, "Where did it go?" My father explained evaporation, and I understood the whole water cycle. It was a successful explanation; my father was a teacher. His explanation of where colors come from was less successful. "Why is the sky blue?" " Because of chemicals", was all I remembered. I continued to treasure my great ambition to discover a new color. I thought I might find it in some exotic place like Africa, in a cave. I knew I would not find it by mixing colors; I had already mixed everything that could be mixed. My mother told me to bury my turtle in the garden and that he would help the flowers grow, and that part of him would be in the flowers, and part of him would go up into the sky to water the flowers.

I decided it was better not to have pets or friends since I couldn't trust myself to take care of them. I recognized my immaturity, and the immaturity all around me, and I knew that no matter how I tried to reach a perfect state beyond the stupidity of my youth, I never would.

Perhaps I have to forgive myself and everyone else, while I try to keep my team alive and victorious. A beautiful fox appears, and in my heart I know he is on my team. I live alone; I have no pets, yet I feel he is my fox from the wooded land around me.

Before accepting death, you have to get used to the idea of old age, it's sort of an icebreaker before meeting your maker.

Today I typed up a journal I kept from one of my first jobs, when I was 16 and 17 years old, saving money to go to Bennington College. I worked in a nursing home:

April 22: The medical aid left me a note of things to do. I guess I misread it because the way I read it, it said: Take Miss Blinko's dentures out. When I went to take them out she wouldn't spit them out. So I reached in to pull them out and her husband asked about it and said she didn't wear dentures. Luckily she still doesn't.

April 23:
"Buck, can you pee, Buck?"
"Heck, yes!"
"Well, pee."
"I'll piss in your face"
Buck's mad…
"Did you Pee?"
"Heck, yes!
"Tootsie—come on, Tootsie, time to get your night gown on."
"I don't want to go."
"We have to Tootsie, come on."
She walks the two-step slowly. She's a retired stripper. If you ask her to she can still shake it. That's what

I've been told. "Lets go back," She says confidentially. She whispers into my ear, "Lets go."

"No, I don't want to go, Tootsie, sit down on the bed. I'll get you a night gown." As I button her pajama top she asks, "Do you like me?" Surprised, I reply, "Yes, I like you, what did you think?"

For a while there isn't much to do so we walk around slowly hand in hand, finally seating ourselves in her usual place. When I go she says, "Why can't you be with me?" She looks worried, but I say I have to go. "We'll see each other later." I say. For the next hours I answer calls from Irene who is paralyzed on the left side and in both legs. Her voice sounds like the whining of a helpless child groping in the dark asking for help, till finally we put her to bed with her rosary.

May 2: It's amazing the constant feeling of danger in a nursing home. Injuries exist like a stretching sand-scape, blowing into new forms, though the situation itself is unchanging. Constant calls for help light red lights in the halls of ever threatening death. There is such uncertainty in life here, and fading, erratic gradations of life until I can hardly distinguish the line before death. I understand how old people depend on routine for security – It's true they can be certain of nothing else but that dinner will be served at 6:00, and their beds will be made in the same certain way.

While I work there, in the home, I find I too have lost all my certainty. Today there was some mix up and the lights kept going off, doors that were always open before were closed. The elevator stopped and I was surprised at the panic I felt. I wondered if someone had died. I trembled and wrung my hands and was so relieved when things were back to normal. I have never known such wretchedness before; the place smells of it. No one here is free of it. The memories of my workday come pouring back when I'm home. While I worked I was very much aware of my physical exhaustion. It was only when it was over, when I came home that I plunged into sorrow; the horror replayed across my eyes. I remember one particular old man. He was as long as the bed - big, tall guy - I didn't like seeing him helpless. There were pictures of him in his youth on the wall. He looked strong and capable then. Now he is in bed at 3:00 p.m., apparently paralyzed, eyes wide as coins, acknowledging nothing.

The perpetual moaning, crying, complaining...as we woke one woman up she was startled, "What's going on?"

"It's time to wake up, Miss Bee," my partner shouts We lift her and put her on a seat with a hole in it and roll her to the toilet.

All the while she is moaning, "I don't have any sense, I don't have any sense. Am I crazy?" We tell her she is not to calm her. It is common here for residents to be distressed about the state of their minds.

Another woman screams, "Someone come talk to me; I'm lost." We have learned that she cannot be helped.

Later however I hear her talking with another lady saying, "Just tell me yes or no; are we in a hospital?"

"No"

"Is Frank here?"

"No"

And so on. She really has no idea where she is; I can't seem to convince her she is in a nursing home. Everyone here is in pain and thinking is very limited by physical wretchedness: yellow swollen feet, purple toes, bedsores, skin ulcers, eyes closed so long they won't open, rectums that don't stay in, drooling, paralysis, asthma, and such lack of muscle that an incredibly large woman weighs only 120 pounds.

I fed one woman that had one arm blown up like a balloon; she always screams at us, " Oh, my god, oh my god, couldn't treat me any rougher, could you?" She demands when we set her on the toilet. She didn't eat much, always haranguing me. I tried to give her water without a straw. "God damn it, pour water all over me, why don't ya. Get that stuff away from me." I tried next to give her some potato soup… "It's slop, that's what, not fit for a dog." I gave her more water. "God damn it there's no reason why I couldn't have cold water." I went to get some ice. I came back, told her what was on her plate, and asked her what she wanted. "Give me a vanilla wafer." After she ate one she always demanded another. I got her to eat some more soup and a few bites of bread. Again she remarked that it wasn't fit for a dog and refused to eat more. When I was finished she said, "Thank you".

So many horrors call back to my memory, till I realized I didn't have tears enough to express the sorrow, the helplessness, wretchedness, uncertainty, and fear of even this one nursing home, much less countless others. As finally I drifted toward sleep, a piece of a song came to mind, "… how sweet the sound that saved a wretch like me…"

May 3: Thank you, thank you, and thank you. I hear it all day long at work after doing little favors for people who can't do for themselves. Occasionally I can't help wondering if someone upstairs is chalking up tallies for me in the good book. When I come home I don't feel as if I've done a thing. I just keep putting them to bed so they can wake up and eat and go to the bathroom and go back to bed. I'd like to take them out of this incubator, stir them up with adventure, ask them about their past, and make them justify their present existence. Is it possible to retrieve the lost part of a mind if that mind cannot be aware of having lost itself?

It seems like I've been working here forever and I have nothing to show for it but my aching back. One of the stresses of this new job is not knowing what is wrong with these people. Their physical peculiarities are never mentioned. One woman is fat on one side of her body and not the other. Why? I don't know. No one else seems to notice. Their excrement looks like ashes. Why? Is no one else curious?

Date unknown: I haven't written about the nursing home in a long time and I doubt I will ever again, so these are my last words on the subject. At first I thought the nursing home was humorous, then sad, now bitter. As a nurse's aid there is no way I can really help anyone and still keep my job. My conscience doesn't like it. It is not right to keep metabolisms going while doing nothing to prevent the tragic way they die. They die confused and helpless with the burden of having failed life in its last stage (maybe I project). Several residents have died since I started working here; for the rest, their time is near. I must ignore this and take my orders from a hardened nurse. She either thinks I'm lazy or dumb. She's always looking for any way to foul me up. She makes it a point to reveal my stupidity or ineptitude. She doesn't want me to work here.

I am discouraged about the whole thing, maybe even about trying to help people. Sometimes I think they're all just lazy cowards not worth my time.

Sometimes I also wonder as I ride my bike home, especially if a dog is chasing me, if I should just make like a resident, and grab a rosary and start chanting the Lord's Prayer while I wait for death's jaws to close.

Thirty years later: I'm not sure what the odds are that my lifetime companion and I will live into old age together. I tried to pick a healthy man who wasn't too much older than me, someone who knows how to take care of himself. Women usually outlive men by thirteen years and usually marry men at least five years older. That means a typical woman has about twenty years without her lifetime companion. If I really accepted death I would accept that I would likely survive my spouse by many years. I am lazy and just think it's a bum deal: that I will have to make the burial/funeral arrangements and then go on living without my best friend and lover. I think I will take up a dangerous sport in my mid-fifties, and try to beat the statistics on widowhood.

I don't have life insurance even though I am very concerned about my children's financial future. I want to give them money while I'm still alive. I don't want to have to make decisions about what happens after I die, decisions about what to do with my body, or even a living will. The mourners will take care of me.

I have to accept the challenges along the way to death; I don't have to face death itself. My task is to transcend death by relying on that self in the pit of my heart that does not die. This hidden self may not be as I hope, but it is all I have to meet my desperate challenges. This word "transcendent" always came up in art school and I could never get a grip on it. How can something be better than what it is? I'm having some dental work done; I'm getting a crown. This is one of my challenges on the way to death; I'm decaying. It's a terrible expense for me, and I realize that body maintenance may become as bad as car maintenance. It seems incredible to me that my challenges, after raising two daughters successfully into adulthood, are not over. I see ahead no mercy on my old age, if it's not one thing it's another. So I see transcendence in meeting life's challenges, that's all. To see the self through it all is transcendence. I think of this grandmother stage of my life as a second life.

My friend had a dog that was dying. The dog moaned and made very evocative sounds like a language. Soon after this dog died he came to me in a dream, and he spoke in his usual way as if trying to form his moans into words and then with great effort he was able to transform his moans into words, he said pushing the words out "ieee dooon't knowww". He was showing me his one great accomplishment. We long for things beyond our reach, and reach them, even a dog can.

As a mother I wonder if there is some co-relation between birth and death. Birth is also a big scary mystery of nature with uncertain outcomes. Will my experience of death be similar to my experience of giving birth? I was so afraid the first time. I wanted so badly to believe it would be painless, even though if you think about it, how could it be? Nonetheless I had a hippie midwife and tried to believe that it was totally natural and therefore beautiful and magical and painless. Even though birth is natural, abortion is always less risky for the mother. I did my homework, but in the end I chose to take the path I was most afraid of. My own mother told me birth had been excruciating. The birth of my first daughter lasted two days, I turned twenty-one the day after she was born, We had decided on a home birth, but if I had known that I would be screaming and moaning so loud I would have gone to the hospital. It is not neighborly to have a home birth. I had never met our upstairs neighbor before, but I went up and showed her what all the screaming was about the next day and I will never forget how heavenly the bread she made and gave to me tasted. It was heaven. I hadn't eaten anything since three days before when I started throwing up, getting the shits, and sweating. My water was the first thing to go. You are supposed to give birth soon after your water breaks but I wasn't dilating. Everything was coming out except the baby. They moved me to the hospital. I had stopped screaming, and started sleeping between contractions. Others seemed worried about me by this time, but I wasn't worried anymore, I had accepted the pain and knew how to take it, I had hit my stride, I just believed that everything was going to be o.k.

I've always looked young for my age until now. I changed my hair and started wearing glasses.

" I like your hair what did you do to it? It makes you look older…"

"I grew out my bangs, when I told my sister I was thinking of doing it she said, it will make you look old"

" It does, it's good to look your age"

I have wrinkles; this is the main way I show my age. I think it's hereditary, one of those things you just can't change, because even though my forehead has been protected all my life from sun, it is very wrinkly. I have cartoon lines of surprise over one eye. Between the ages of 40 and 42 I enjoyed hearing that I looked too young to be the mother of college age daughters. Now almost 43, I know that I look my age. It seems like a sudden unpleasant award. Looking young was not pleasant for most of my adult life, or even as a child. Looking too young to be pushing a baby carriage, too young to be a teacher, too young to be taken seriously was not fun. Sometimes I'm o.k. with my wrinkled face, my signs of age. Sometimes I do feel proud of my battle scars, just like the stretch marks on my belly and thighs that are the price I gladly paid for my daughters.

I see myself as being in the grandmother stage of life, though it seems sudden. I think of my life ahead as a bonus life, a life beyond natural allotment, beyond the successful breeding and rearing of my young. Women experience dramatic and mysterious body changes that are on par with death itself. If I try to apply what I've learned as a woman about the mandatory metamorphosis humans go though I would surmise that death will be everything you have heard it will be, but that you will come to terms with it anyway, miraculously so.

Through the creative link of influence we can see into other worlds. I felt the influence of the personality in my womb with both my pregnancies and I think the little fetuses had some idea of who I was too. I mentioned that I screamed a lot in my first pregnancy; well it is no wonder that my first-born is very vocal. As a newborn she was already singing. She was an early talker; she made up words we understood right off. We predicted she would be a lawyer because she was verbose and persuasive. She has influenced me to become a better negotiator. One of her favorite foods is potato, which was my favorite food during pregnancy. My second born had effect on me while I was pregnant with her. I felt beautiful and confident in a way I had never felt before. I modeled for art classes while I was pregnant with her. I felt sure the feeling of beauty and confidence were somehow coming from her. This daughter turned out to be especially beautiful, and has helped me along my path by encouraging me; somehow I have always felt her support. She is quiet, I didn't scream during her birth. The birth was long, but not as long. Again I was taken to the hospital. There was a picture covering the whole wall opposite me of the ocean waves coming into shore. This picture was extremely calming for me. I felt ready and I pushed hard but the baby wouldn't come. I caught the eye of a doctor walking past our door, not my doctor, and he reached in and pushed back the baby's arm so that she could get out headfirst. Then she came right out and they placed her on my chest and she just held on to my finger for a while. She is the one who can concentrate; I could always see this on her brow. She can go with the flow and find serendipity, the way the strange doctor instantly seemed to know what to do and did it. The influence between parents and children flows both ways.

I dreamed that a dead baby fell out of my shopping cart; it had been there unknown to me for some time under the blankets. When I picked up the baby it opened one eye and looked at me. Then it spoke as if it were a grown up,

"Well, now that you have found me are you ready for the responsibility?"

I said, "Yes." What else could I say, the baby was looking alive and well now and it had no one else to take care of him.

Then the baby said, "Give me back to my mother"

"Where is your mother?" I asked

"The cart is my mother." The baby said

I think beauty is the eternal thing and that is why women never want to let go of it. My grandmother's big regret was that she lost her girlish figure. I think it's that will to hold on to beauty that is really beautiful, and I believe where there's a will there's a way. "Cuteness is all that lasts," I said seeing my first-born.

At the foot of my bed there is a picture painted by my grandmother. It is a loose black ink painting of a landscape. I see her in the nude diving into the mountains on the map of where she went after death. It was painted in the year of my birth. I acquired it at a tag sale. I took it and framed it. The framer who had also framed some of my artwork said he could see the family sense of line and how it was reassuring, to see where things come from.

When I lose something I know it has only gone to the lost world, joining my red rubber ball that the lost world was invented or discovered for. It is an odd sort of heaven for objects – though I imagine it as white space. I bounced the ball and it disappeared.

Conclusion

Phrases to Use For Spiritual Self Help

Despite everything, I always thought and still believe you are a great artist, and that I always have been and still am proud that you are my....

I'm sorry for my inappropriate comment.

What did you mean when you said...?

Oh. Thanks.

I want to reassure you that I wouldn't ....I was only joking when I said that.

How are ..., should I drop them a note? If so where are they?

Maybe the sickness was caused by...try...

Not at all, I'm happy to do it.

We'll just have to see how this plays out.

It's not stupid it's your dream.

You always have what I need.

How was your week, your day?

Thanks for listening.

Thanks for your thoughts.

Thanks for saving my ass.

Thanks for your honesty.

If this unlucky thing hadn't happened, this lucky thing wouldn't have happened. See?

Let me tick off a few of the reasons I think you're great...

Don't worry about it.

At least we still have...

It's not that bad, it looks like it's supposed to be that way.

Do we know each other from ...?

You can borrow our garden cart anytime.

If you get yourself in a bind, call me.

Hello sunshine.

If it doesn't get any worse I think I can take it.

I love you.

There's no answer like the no answer, it's the only answer I know.

Yes.

What is the ultimate truth?

My life is like a melody.

I can survive anything.

I like to wear the bonnet with the button on the back.

She can do anything.

That's a great idea.

You are so smart!

Maybe you're not a flubber upper.

Let me know if you have any questions or concerns, please let me know!

I love nature.

If spirits didn't exist your body couldn't move.

If you don't believe me go ask yourself.

Babies are very powerful, they can control their world with just their feelings.

All thinking is wishful.

www.ingramcontent.com/pod-product-compliance
Lightning Source LLC
Chambersburg PA
CBHW031631160426
43196CB00006B/369